A Study of Bahá'u'lláh's Tablet to the Christians

by

Michael W. Sours

ONEWORLD
OXFORD

A Study of
Bahá'u'lláh's Tablet to the
Christians

Oneworld Publications Ltd
185 Banbury Road, Oxford, OX2 7AR

© Michael Sours 1990
All rights reserved. Copyright under Berne Convention

British Library Cataloguing in Publication Data
Sours, Michael W.
A Study of Bahá'u'lláh's Tablet to the Christians
1. Bahá'í Faith. Bahá'u'lláh 1817–1892
I. Title
823'. 914 [F]

ISBN 1-85168-016-X (hardcover)
ISBN 1-85168-017-9 (softcover)

Typeset by DMD Ltd, St. Clements, Oxford
Printed and bound in Great Britain
by Biddles Ltd, Guildford and King's Lynn

*'Let the Breeze of God awaken you.
Verily, it hath wafted over the world.'*

BAHÁ'U'LLÁH

CONTENTS

PREFACE	1
INTRODUCTION	3
THE *LAWḤ-I-AQDAS*	15
THE *LAWḤ-I-AQDAS* WITH COMMENTARY AND NOTES	27
GLOSSARY OF ABBREVIATIONS	191
BIBLIOGRAPHY	193
INDEX TO BIBLE REFERENCES	198
GENERAL INDEX	202

PREFACE

I would like to acknowledge gratefully my debt to the many individuals whose practical assistance or encouragement helped to bring this book to publication.

I would especially like to thank Stephen Lambden, who read the manuscript and made many helpful suggestions and corrections. Many of his comments raised new issues. In subsequent correspondence he took the time to answer carefully a series of questions involving the original Arabic. With the information that he, and later another Bahá'í scholar, Dr Iraj Rabbani, provided, I was able to consider more accurately the relationship between some of Bahá'u'lláh's terminology and the Bible. Because of the complexity of the issues I have tried not to bring our discussions into the commentary itself, but the issues raised were nevertheless important in shaping some of the conclusions. Because Stephen Lambden conveyed his comments and suggestions in writing, I have occasionally quoted from his letters in the footnotes. However, any errors in my final conclusions are my own and should not be attributed to either Stephen Lambden or Dr Iraj Rabbani.

M.W.S.

INTRODUCTION

BAHÁ'U'LLÁH

The Faith of Bahá'u'lláh has its origins in the religious movement founded by Siyyid 'Alí-Muḥammad, or 'the Báb', meaning 'the Gate'. In 1844 the Báb began a ministry which initiated a new religion and sought to prepare the way for the appearance of One who would fulfil the Scriptures of all past religions. However, His movement met with violent opposition from the Islamic clergy and government of Persia (Iran), many of the Báb's followers were killed, He was imprisoned, and in 1850 He was publicly executed.

Bahá'u'lláh was a supporter of the Báb, though it is believed that they never met. In 1852, during severe persecution of the Báb's followers, Bahá'u'lláh was imprisoned in Ṭihrán, Persia, and then exiled to Baghdád. Bahá'u'lláh assumed the leadership of the Bábí community, and in 1863 He announced to His followers that He was the One whom the Báb had foretold. That same year He was banished further to the city of Constantinople[1] and later to Adrianople.[2] During Bahá'u'lláh's exile in Adrianople (1863–8), He composed many tablets, among which was one directed to the kings of the world (Súriy-i-Mulúk), one to the ruler of Persia

---

1. Present-day Istanbul. The name Constantinople comes from Constantine, the first ruler of the Roman Empire to accept Christianity (AD 312).

2. Adrianople, present-day Edirne, was at that time a city within the Ottoman Empire.

(*Lawḥ-i-Sulṭán*),[3] and His first tablet to Napoleon III. In these tablets Bahá'u'lláh sets out His claims and warns the world's rulers that unless they change direction, reduce their armaments, act peacefully towards one another and respect the rights of their subjects, a 'Divine chastisement shall assail you from every direction and the sentence of His justice shall be pronounced against you'.

In 1868 He and His companions were exiled to 'Akká[4] and imprisoned. While still considered a prisoner, Bahá'u'lláh was released from prison two years later and took up residence first in 'Akká and later in the surrounding area, where He remained under virtual house arrest until His passing in 1892. During this period Bahá'u'lláh wrote tablets to the rulers of the Christian nations, then the most powerful nations on earth: Czar Alexander II, Queen Victoria, Emperor Franz-Josef of Austro-Hungary, and Kaiser Wilhelm I of Prussia, and a second tablet to Emperor Napoleon III. He also wrote a tablet to Pope Pius IX. Finally, among His last tablets was the *Lawḥ-i-Aqdas* (The Most Holy Tablet), commonly known as the Tablet to the Christians.[5]

THE *LAWḤ-I-AQDAS*

It is not known for which individual this tablet was originally written. There is, however, some speculation that it was revealed in honour of a Syrian, Faris Effendi, who converted to the Bahá'í Faith. However, Adib Taherzadeh

---

3. Although this tablet was written in Adrianople, it was delivered later from 'Akká. A believer, a youth of 17, personally delivered the tablet to Náṣiri'd-Dín S͟háh and was consequently tortured to death (Adib Taherzadeh, *The Revelation of Bahá'u'lláh*, vol. III, pp. 176–203).
4. Now a port city in Israel, in the nineteenth century 'Akká was a penal colony within the Turkish Empire.
5. See Shoghi Effendi, *GPB* p. 216. This tablet should not be confused with the better known *Kitáb-i-Aqdas* (The Most Holy Book), which contains 'the basic laws and ordinances on which the fabric of His future World Order must rest' (*GPB* p. 213).

INTRODUCTION

writes: 'There is so far no conclusive evidence to prove this. All we can say is that possibly he was the recipient of this Tablet.'[6]

The tablet is written in Arabic, and it is certain that parts were translated into English at least as early as 1904, if not earlier.[7] A few years later a complete English translation was published in an early Bahá'í periodical called *Star of the West*,[8] and separately as *Lawh el Akdas: The Holy Tablet*.[9] In 1923 the *Lawh-i-Aqdas* was published under the title, *Tablet to the Christians*.[10] Better translations of selected portions of the tablet were later made by Shoghi Effendi and these appear in his book *The Promised Day is Come* (1941). The remaining portions were also re-translated later, and these appeared together with those made by Shoghi Effendi in their entirety in the compilation entitled *Tablets of Bahá'u'lláh* (1978). It is this latest translation that has been used throughout this book.

In some respects, it can be said that the message of the tablet in fact predates its actual writing, as the *Lawh-i-Aqdas* is largely a reaffirmation of truths Bahá'u'lláh had previously proclaimed. Even as early as 1862, in the *Kitáb-i-Íqán*, although this was not written as a direct proclamation of His mission, one finds the essential arguments and exegetical approach later used in the *Lawh-i-Aqdas*. The core of the *Lawh-i-Aqdas*, Bahá'u'lláh's proclamation to Christians, His allusions to biblical prophecies, His counsels, admonitions, and spiritual assurances to those who believe, were all repeatedly expounded by His followers from the earliest times, and

---

6. See Adib Taherzadeh, *The Revelation of Bahá'u'lláh*, vol. IV, pp. 227. An account of the conversion of Fáris Effendi is given in vol. III, pp. 5–11.

7. Some excerpts can be found, for example, in *Bahá'í Martyrdoms in Persia*, a reprint of an earlier 1904 publication. It was written by Ḥájí Mírzá Ḥaydar-'Alí at the request of 'Abdu'l-Bahá.

8. See vol. IV, no. 1, 21 March 1913, pp. 14–15, 19–20.

9. Chicago Bahá'í Publishing Society, 1913.

10. See *Bahá'í Scriptures. Selections from the Utterances of Bahá'u'lláh and 'Abdu'l-Bahá*, ed. Horace Holley, 2nd edn, pp. 124–30.

later, most notably by 'Abdu'l-Bahá, Bahá'u'lláh's son, in the many talks He delivered in Europe and America.

The title 'The Most Holy Tablet' suggests that this tablet must have a particularly great significance, but why Bahá'u'lláh chose to call it 'Most Holy' is not entirely clear, and there remains some uncertainty as to how much can be correctly inferred from the title. We do know, however, that Shoghi Effendi ranked the Lawḥ-i-Aqdas among the tablets which constituted the 'choicest fruits' of Bahá'u'lláh's Revelation, and which 'mark the consummation of His [Bahá'u'lláh's] forty-year-long ministry' (GPB 216).

It is only speculation, but the title may have been given to emphasize the importance of Bahá'u'lláh's message as it pertains to the role Christians will play in the spreading and establishment of His Cause. The Messianic expectations of the Christians have been strong and enduring. Bahá'u'lláh claims to be no less than the fulfilment of those expectations. The reception of Bahá'u'lláh's Faith in His own country and in the Islamic world in general was similar to that accorded Christ by the Jews. Even as the torch of faith was relayed to the Greeks by the few receptive Jews of Christ's day, in this age it may be the Christians who take a leading role in carrying Bahá'u'lláh's teachings and 'Glad-Tidings' throughout the world. The efforts of countless believers from the land of the birth of the Bahá'í Faith, efforts which can only be described as truly heroic and sacrificial, appear to have already firmly carried that torch to the peoples of the West.

The content of Bahá'u'lláh's tablet to the Christians consists chiefly of interweaving themes – He warns Christians not to make the same mistake in judging Him as the Pharisees made in judging Christ. He states that He has suffered for the sake of the world, that He is the same Spirit as Christ, and that the promises of Christ's return, foretold in the Scriptures, have been fulfilled in Him. He praises Christ, calls for Christians to arise to proclaim His Cause, predicts the downfall of Christian leaders, and assures the blessings of those who have acknowledged

INTRODUCTION

and remained steadfast in His Cause.

Much of the terminology and other aspects of Bahá'u'lláh's writings clearly reflect both His cultural background and religious heritage.[11] Regardless of how timeless the inspiration may be in any of the world's Scriptures, it must be admitted that the outer form is always influenced by the specific cultural environment of the time in which they were written. For example, in the New Testament we find stories, places, people and Judaic terminology that were a part of the culture of that time. Just as Christianity grew out of the Judaic tradition, so both of these great religions contributed to the Islamic heritage. Thus the Qur'án, the holy Book of the Muslims, makes frequent use of biblical terminology and narrative to convey its message. This is due not only to shared geography but also to the fact that the Qur'án affirms the divine origins of Judaism and Christianity.

Not surprisingly, one finds this heritage reflected in Bahá'u'lláh's writings. Although Bahá'ís believe His teachings are addressed to all people, they are nevertheless expressed in the religious terminology of western religious tradition.[12] Anyone familiar with the Bible will readily sense from the terminology of the *Lawḥ-i-Aqdas* that Bahá'u'lláh is drawing from an ancient river of spiritual tradition. Moreover, the style of the English translation of the tablet, like all of Bahá'u'lláh's writings, is in some respects similar to that of the Authorized, King James' version of the Bible.[13]

---

11. Adib Taherzadeh discusses this point briefly in *The Revelation of Bahá'u'lláh*, vol. I, pp. 21–2.

12. Western, in contrast to the terminology common to Far Eastern religions, such as Hinduism and Buddhism.

13. At this time there has been very little written in English in the way of scholarly appraisals of Bahá'u'lláh's literary style. However, E. G. Browne writes, 'The Babis and Baha'is have developed a somewhat distinctive style of their own in Persian which possesses considerable merits. Some of Bahá'u'lláh's "Tablets" (Alwah) addressed to Zoroastrian inquirers are even written in pure Persian without admixture of Arabic. Their most important works, like the *Kitáb-i-Aqdas* ("The Most Holy Book"), are, however, written in Arabic. From the point of view of style, both in Persian and Arabic, an immense improvement was effected by Bahá'u'lláh', *A Literary History of Persia*, vol. IV, p. 423.

This similarity of style, coupled with the fact that there are so many allusions to the Scriptures of the Bible and such a strong use of biblical terminology, merits further comment. It should be emphasized that by using earlier Scriptures as the basis of theological argument and instruction, Bahá'u'lláh is affirming the authority of those Scriptures. This approach can be found not only in the Qur'án but also in the New Testament itself and is even apparent in the discourses of Jesus, which frequently employed references to and explanations of verses in the Old Testament.[14]

Inevitably some people will be compelled to ask: is the familiarity one senses between the words and methods of one Prophet and the Prophets who came before Him, evidence of imitation, or is it the voice of the same God?[15] Or from a Christian point of view, one might ask: is Bahá'u'lláh the Shepherd whose voice Christ said His sheep would recognize?[16] This is a matter of faith that one must resolve for oneself. And, perhaps it should be added, it is also a matter of justice and wisdom to enquire first, before judging. What seems certain is that Bahá'u'lláh used biblical Scripture and terminology in the Lawḥ-i-Aqdas to convey a clear message about the relationship between His Cause and that of Christ. Their use also reveals Bahá'u'lláh's interpretation of the intended meaning of these biblical passages.

14. *The Cambridge History of the Bible.* vol. 1, *From the Beginnings to Jerome,* p. 377.
15. The historian Will Durant writes concerning Christ: 'Were these moral ideas new? Nothing is new except arrangement. The central theme of Christ's preaching – the coming Judgment and Kingdom – was already a century old among the Jews. The Law had long since inculcated brotherhood: "Thou shalt love thy neighbor as thyself," said Leviticus; even "the stranger that dwelleth with you shall be unto you as one born among you, and thou shalt love him as thyself." Exodus had commanded the Jews to do good to their enemies: a good Jew will restore the straying ox or ass even of the "enemy that hateth thee." The prophets, too, had ranked a good life above all ritual; and Isaiah and Hosea had begun to change Yahveh from a Lord of Hosts into a God of Love. Hillel, like Confucius, had phrased the Golden Rule. We must not hold it against Jesus that he inherited and used the rich moral lore of his people.' *Caesar and Christ,* p. 567.
16. John 10:4.

In the Lawḥ-i-Aqdas, Bahá'u'lláh quotes from and alludes to Bible passages in a way that indicates a broad interpretive approach. He reveals a consistent pattern of biblical symbolism that diverges from many of the literal interpretations of traditional Christianity.[17] This divergence is given emphasis in the way He unfolds His own message with the use of metaphorical and symbolic language. Occasionally He even delivers His message in the form of allegorical and mystic dialogues – first with 'the Son', 'the Burning Bush', and 'Bethlehem', and then with 'Mount Sinai'. Such passages, like many of His writings, defy any attempt to limit His words to one outward meaning. The terminology often embraces important themes that can be traced through the Bible from the beginning of the Old Testament to the Book of Revelation. In this way Bahá'u'lláh places His Revelation in the context of the Bible and the eschatological hopes of our age, without employing lengthy and limiting explanations.

THE COMMENTARY

The purpose of this commentary is to bring together notes, observations and explanations that will help foster a better understanding of the tablet's most basic messages. The commentary also includes explanations intended to help Christians understand how Bahá'ís generally interpret Scripture, particularly some well-known Bible prophecies.

---

17. Bahá'u'lláh speaks at length in the Kitáb-i-Íqán (The Book of Certitude) concerning the correct approach to the interpretation of Scripture. He urges people to reconsider and reject some age-old interpretations, arguing that such traditional views do not adequately reflect the nature of God, especially His all-encompassing love and grace. Specific examples and explanations, especially of biblical prophetic terminology, can be found throughout most of Part 1 (e.g. pp. 18–93). For the purpose of symbolic terms, see pp. 49 and 254–5. The scriptural meaning of sovereignty and related terminology, as well as the meaning of 'divine Presence' and 'return', are the focus of Part 2, pp. 97–257.

It is of course presumptuous to write a commentary on the *Lawḥ-i-Aqdas*. Much of what is said can be no more than speculation about the Author's intentions, and each reader may understand some aspects of it in a different way. Moreover, while the commentary may bring out some aspects suggested by the text, it is of course possible to miss the real substance while drawing attention to a minor theme. Some passages are certainly open to broader interpretation than could ever be fully expounded in one simple commentary. Readers should therefore not limit themselves to the explanations given or accept them without question.

Some readers will no doubt already be acquainted with many of the details explained, but there may be others who are unfamiliar with the Bible or the Bahá'í Faith. The commentary tries to take account of this. Sometimes points are brought up which will seem at odds with the doctrinal views of some Christians. In such instances an effort has been made briefly to include Bahá'í explanations that may be of interest to Christians, but occasionally such issues have had to be left out to avoid disrupting the flow of the commentary. More information is available in other books specifically directed at resolving these issues (see the bibliography).

The views expressed in this commentary do not represent an official Bahá'í understanding of the *Lawḥ-i-Aqdas*. In fact, it is one of the admirable teachings of the Bahá'í Faith that individual believers are free to interpret the sacred texts for themselves, although it is not permissible to insist that others must accept such a personal view as authoritative. Interpretation in the Bahá'í community is encouraged in a spirit of tolerance for the views of others, and mindful that to cause dissension or disunity is the antithesis of Bahá'u'lláh's teachings.[18]

---

18. 'A clear distinction is made in our Faith between authoritative interpretation and the interpretation or understanding that each individual arrives at for himself from his study of its teachings. While the former is confined to the Guardian, the latter, according to the guidance given to us by the Guardian himself, should by no means be suppressed. In fact such individual interpret-

The full text as it appeared in the 1978 English translation is arranged, like almost all Bahá'í texts, in conventional paragraph form, without any system of verse numbering such as those found typically in the Bible or the Qur'án. To facilitate this commentary, the text has been numbered according to paragraph and sentence. Perhaps one day editions of Bahá'í Scriptures will be available numbered by verse.[19] Readers are strongly recommended to read through the Lawḥ-i-Aqdas first, without the commentary, in order to experience the flow of verses free of interruption and the influence of outside opinions.

---

ation is considered the fruit of man's rational power and conducive to a better understanding of the teachings, provided that no disputes or arguments arise among the friends and the individual himself understands and makes it clear that his views are merely his own.' The Universal House of Justice, *Wellspring of Guidance: Messages from The Universal House of Justice, 1963–1968*, p. 88.

19. The original Arabic of the Lawḥ-i-Aqdas is not divided into either paragraphs or verses. The English translation in its choice of sentence lengths and paragraphs is in large measure a matter of interpretation.

THE LAWḤ-I-AQDAS
(The Most Holy Tablet)

I   *This is the Most Holy Tablet sent down from the holy kingdom unto the one who hath set his face towards the Object of the adoration of the world, He Who hath come from the heaven of eternity, invested with transcendent glory.*

    In the name of the Lord, the Lord of great glory.

II   This is an Epistle from Our presence unto him whom the veils of names have failed to keep back from God, the Creator of earth and heaven, that his eyes may be cheered in the days of his Lord, the Help in Peril, the Self-Subsisting.

III   Say, O followers of the Son! Have ye shut out yourselves from Me by reason of My Name? Wherefore ponder ye not in your hearts? Day and night ye have been calling upon your Lord, the Omnipotent, but when He came from the heaven of eternity in His great glory, ye turned aside from Him and remained sunk in heedlessness.

IV   Consider those who rejected the Spirit when He came unto them with manifest dominion. How numerous the Pharisees who had secluded themselves in synagogues in His name, lamenting over their separation from Him, and yet when the portals of reunion were flung open and the divine Luminary shone resplendent from the Dayspring of Beauty, they disbelieved in God, the Exalted, the Mighty. They failed to attain His presence, notwithstanding that His advent had been promised them in the Book of Isaiah as well as in the Books of the Prophets and the Messengers. No one from among them turned his face towards the Dayspring of divine bounty except such as were destitute of any power amongst men. And yet, today, every man endowed with power and invested with sovereignty prideth himself on His Name. Moreover, call thou to mind the one who sentenced Jesus to death. He was the most learned of His age in His own country, whilst he who was only a fisherman believed in Him. Take good heed and be of them that observe the warning.

V   Consider likewise, how numerous at this time are the monks who have secluded themselves in their churches, calling upon the Spirit, but when He appeared through the power of Truth, they failed to draw nigh unto Him and are numbered with those that have gone far astray. Happy are they that have abandoned them and set their faces towards Him Who is the Desire of all that are in the heavens and all that are on the earth.

VI   They read the Evangel and yet refuse to acknowledge the All-Glorious Lord, notwithstanding that He hath come through the potency of His exalted, His mighty and gracious dominion. We, verily, have come for your sakes, and have borne the misfortunes of the world for your salvation. Flee ye the One Who hath sacrificed His life that ye may be quickened? Fear God, O followers of the Spirit, and walk not in the footsteps of every divine that hath gone far astray. Do ye imagine that He seeketh His own interests, when He hath, at all times, been threatened by the swords of the enemies; or that He seeketh the vanities of the world, after He hath been imprisoned in the most desolate of cities? Be fair in your judgement and follow not the footsteps of the unjust.

VII Open the doors of your hearts. He Who is the Spirit verily standeth before them. Wherefore keep ye afar from Him Who hath purposed to draw you nigh unto a Resplendent Spot? Say: We, in truth, have opened unto you the gates of the Kingdom. Will ye bar the doors of your houses in My face? This indeed is naught but a grievous error. He, verily, hath again come down from heaven, even as He came down from it the first time. Beware lest ye dispute that which He proclaimeth, even as the people before you disputed His utterances. Thus instructeth you the True One, could ye but perceive it.

VIII The river Jordan is joined to the Most Great Ocean, and the Son, in the holy vale, crieth out: 'Here am I, here am I, O Lord, my God!', whilst Sinai circleth round the House, and the Burning Bush calleth aloud: 'He Who is the Desired One is come in His transcendent majesty.' Say, Lo! The Father is come, and that which ye were promised in the Kingdom is fulfilled! This is the Word which the Son concealed, when to those around Him He said: 'Ye cannot bear it now.' And when the appointed time was fulfilled and the Hour had struck, the Word shone forth above the horizon of the Will of God. Beware, O followers of the Son, that ye cast it not behind your backs. Take ye fast hold of it. Better is this for you than all that ye possess. Verily He is nigh unto them that do good. The Hour which We had concealed from the knowledge of the peoples of the earth and of the favoured angels hath come to pass. Say, verily, He hath testified of Me, and I do testify of Him. Indeed, He hath purposed no one other than Me. Unto this beareth witness every fair-minded and understanding soul.

IX Though beset with countless afflictions, We summon the people unto God, the Lord of names. Say, strive ye to attain that which ye have been promised in the Books of God, and walk not in the way of the ignorant. My body hath endured imprisonment that ye may be released from the bondage of self. Set your faces then towards His countenance and follow not the footsteps of every hostile oppressor. Verily, He hath consented to be sorely abased that ye may attain unto glory, and yet, ye are disporting yourselves in the vale of heedlessness. He, in truth, liveth in the most desolate of abodes for your sakes, whilst ye dwell in your palaces.

X   Say, did ye not hearken to the Voice of the Crier, calling aloud in the wilderness of the Bayán, bearing unto you the glad tidings of the coming of your Lord, the All-Merciful? Lo! He is come in the sheltering shadow of Testimony, invested with conclusive proof and evidence, and those who truly believe in Him regard His presence as the embodiment of the Kingdom of God. Blessed is the man who turneth towards Him, and woe betide such as deny or doubt Him.

XI   Announce thou unto the priests: Lo! He Who is the Ruler is come. Step out from behind the veil in the name of thy Lord, He Who layeth low the necks of all men. Proclaim then unto all mankind the glad-tidings of this mighty, this glorious Revelation. Verily, He Who is the Spirit of Truth is come to guide you unto all truth. He speaketh not as prompted by His own self, but as bidden by Him Who is the All-Knowing, the All-Wise.

XII   Say, this is the One Who hath glorified the Son and hath exalted His Cause. Cast away, O peoples of the earth, that which ye have and take fast hold of that which ye are bidden by the All-Powerful, He Who is the Bearer of the Trust of God. Purge ye your ears and set your hearts towards Him that ye may hearken to the most wondrous Call which hath been raised from Sinai, the habitation of your Lord, the Most Glorious. It will, in truth, draw you nigh unto the Spot wherein ye will perceive the splendour of the light of His countenance which shineth above this luminous Horizon.

XIII O concourse of priests! Leave the bells, and come forth, then, from your churches. It behoveth you, in this day, to proclaim aloud the Most Great Name among the nations. Prefer ye to be silent, whilst every stone and every tree shouteth aloud: 'The Lord is come in His great glory!'? Well is it with the man who hasteneth unto him. Verily, he is numbered among them whose names will be eternally recorded and who will be mentioned by the Concourse on High. Thus hath it been decreed by the Spirit in this wondrous Tablet. He that summoneth men in My name is, verily, of Me, and he will show forth that which is beyond the power of all that are on earth. Follow ye the Way of the Lord and walk not in the footsteps of them that are sunk in heedlessness. Well is it with the slumberer who is stirred by the Breeze of God and ariseth from amongst the dead, directing his steps towards the Way of the Lord. Verily, such a man is regarded, in the sight of God, the True One, as a jewel amongst men and is reckoned with the blissful.

XIV Say: In the East the Light of His Revelation hath broken; in the West the signs of His dominion have appeared. Ponder this in your hearts, O people, and be not of those who grievously erred when My Remembrance came unto them at the bidding of the Almighty, the All-Praised. Let the Breeze of God awaken you. Verily, it hath wafted over the world. Well is it with him that hath discovered the fragrance thereof and been accounted among the well-assured.

XV O concourse of bishops! Ye are the stars of the heaven of My knowledge. My mercy desireth not that ye should fall upon the earth. My justice, however, declareth: 'This is that which the Son hath decreed.' And whatsoever hath proceeded out of His blameless, His truth-speaking, trustworthy mouth, can never be altered. The bells, verily, peal out My Name, and lament over Me, but My spirit rejoiceth with evident gladness. The body of the Loved One yearneth for the cross, and His head is eager for the spear, in the path of the All-Merciful. The ascendancy of the oppressor can in no wise deter Him from His purpose. We have summoned all created things to attain the presence of thy Lord, the King of all names. Blessed is the man that hath set his face towards God, the Lord of the Day of Reckoning.

XVI O concourse of monks! If ye choose to follow Me, I will make you heirs of My Kingdom; and if ye transgress against Me, I will, in My long-suffering, endure it patiently, and I, verily, am the Ever-Forgiving, the All-Merciful.

XVII O land of Syria! What hath become of thy righteousness? Thou art, in truth, ennobled by the footsteps of thy Lord. Hast thou perceived the fragrance of heavenly reunion, or art thou to be accounted of the heedless?

XVIII Bethlehem is astir with the Breeze of God. We hear her voice saying: 'O most generous Lord! Where is Thy great glory established? The sweet savours of Thy presence have quickened me, after I had melted in my separation from Thee. Praised be Thou in that Thou hast raised the veils, and come with power in evident glory.' We called unto her from behind the Tabernacle of Majesty and Grandeur: 'O Bethlehem!

This Light hath risen in the orient, and travelled towards the occident, until it reached thee in the evening of its life. Tell Me then: Do the sons recognize the Father, and acknowledge Him, or do they deny Him, even as the people aforetime denied Him?' Whereupon she cried out saying: 'Thou art, in truth, the All-Knowing, the Best-Informed.' Verily, We behold all created things moved to bear witness unto Us. Some know Us and bear witness, while the majority bear witness, yet know Us not.

XIX Mount Sinai is astir with the joy of beholding Our countenance. She hath lifted her enthralling voice in glorification of her Lord, saying: 'O Lord! I sense the fragrance of Thy garment. Methinks Thou art near, invested with the signs of God. Thou hast ennobled these regions with Thy footsteps. Great is the blessedness of Thy people, could they but know Thee and inhale Thy sweet savours; and woe betide them that are fast asleep.'

XX Happy art thou who hast turned thy face towards My countenance, inasmuch as thou hast rent the veils asunder, hast shattered the idols and recognized thine eternal Lord. The people of the Qur'án have risen up against Us without any clear proof or evidence, tormenting Us at every moment with a fresh torment. They idly imagine that tribulations can frustrate Our Purpose. Vain indeed is that which they have imagined. Verily, thy Lord is the One Who ordaineth whatsoever He pleaseth.

XXI I never passed a tree but Mine heart addressed it saying: 'O would that thou wert cut down in My name, and My body crucified upon thee.' We revealed this passage in the Epistle to the Sháh that it might serve as a warning to the followers of religions. Verily, thy Lord is the All-Knowing, the All-Wise.

XXII Let not the things they have perpetrated grieve thee. Truly they are even as dead, and not living. Leave them unto the dead, then turn thy face towards Him Who is the Life-Giver of the world. Beware lest the sayings of the heedless sadden thee. Be thou steadfast in the Cause, and teach the people with consummate wisdom. Thus enjoineth thee the Ruler of earth and heaven. He is in truth the Almighty, the Most Generous. Erelong will God exalt thy remembrance and will inscribe with the Pen of Glory that which thou didst utter for the sake of His love. He is in truth the Protector of the doers of good.

XXIII Give My remembrance to the one named Murád and say: 'Blessed art thou, O Murád, inasmuch as thou didst cast away the promptings of thine own desire and hast followed Him Who is the Desire of all mankind.'

XXIV Say: Blessed the slumberer who is awakened by My Breeze. Blessed the lifeless one who is quickened through My reviving breaths. Blessed the eye that is solaced by gazing at My beauty. Blessed the wayfarer who directeth his steps towards the Tabernacle of My glory and majesty. Blessed the distressed one who seeketh refuge beneath the shadow of My canopy. Blessed the sore athirst who hasteneth to the soft-flowing waters of My loving-kindness. Blessed the insatiate soul who casteth away his selfish desires for love of Me and taketh his place at the banquet table which I have sent down from the heaven of divine bounty for My chosen ones. Blessed the abased one who layeth fast hold on the cord of My glory; and the needy one who entereth beneath the shadow of the Tabernacle of My wealth. Blessed the ignorant one who seeketh the fountain of My knowledge; and the heedless one who cleaveth to the cord of My remembrance. Blessed the soul that hath been raised to life through My quickening breath and hath gained admittance into My heavenly Kingdom. Blessed the man whom the sweet savours of reunion with Me have stirred and caused to draw nigh unto the Dayspring of My Revelation. Blessed the ear that hath heard and the tongue that hath borne witness and the eye that hath seen and recognized the Lord Himself, in His great glory and majesty, invested with grandeur and dominion. Blessed are they that have attained His presence. Blessed the man who hath sought enlightenment from the Day-Star of My Word. Blessed he who hath attired his head with the diadem of My love. Blessed is he who hath heard of My grief and hath arisen to aid Me among My people. Blessed is he who hath laid down his life in My path and hath borne manifold hardships for the sake of My Name. Blessed the man who, assured of My Word, hath arisen from among the dead to celebrate My praise. Blessed is he that hath been enraptured by My wondrous melodies and hath rent the veils asunder through the potency of My might. Blessed is he who hath remained faithful to My Covenant, and whom the things of the world have not kept back from attaining My Court of holiness. Blessed is the man who hath detached himself from all else but Me, hath soared in the atmosphere of My love, hath gained admittance into My Kingdom, gazed upon My realms of glory, quaffed the living waters of My bounty, hath drunk his fill from the heavenly river of My loving providence, acquainted himself with My Cause, apprehended that which I concealed within the treasury of My Words, and hath shone forth from the horizon of divine knowledge engaged in My praise and glorification. Verily, he is of Me. Upon him rest My mercy, My loving-kindness, My bounty and My glory.

THE LAWḤ-I-AQDAS
with Commentary and Notes

I

1 This is the Most Holy Tablet[20] sent down from the holy kingdom unto the one who hath set his face towards the Object of the adoration of the world, He Who hath come from the heaven of eternity, invested with transcendent glory.

In the name of the Lord, the Lord of great glory.

COMMENTARY

This opening passage serves as Bahá'u'lláh's own introduction to the Lawḥ-i-Aqdas. In it He refers to the person in honour of whom this tablet was written, boldly identifies Himself as One Who has been appointed by the authority of God, and also makes the claim that this tablet is written with God's authority.

The tablet is directed at 'the *one who hath set his face* towards the Object of the adoration of the world' (emphasis added). This may mean generally, any person who has believed in Bahá'u'lláh,[21] or it may be a specific reference to the individual for whom this tablet was originally written.

The phrase, 'the Object of the adoration of the world', is

---

20. Why this is called the 'Most Holy Tablet' is explained in the Introduction, p. 8.
21. Cf. XX:1.

a title which Bahá'u'lláh uses to refer to Himself.[22] This title, like each of the phrases of the opening passage, asserts the claim that Bahá'u'lláh Himself is appointed by the authority of God, and that this tablet is divinely inspired. This assertion is set forth by the use of symbolic imagery typical of the Bible. Bahá'u'lláh states that the tablet is 'sent down from the holy kingdom', and that He has 'come from the heaven of eternity'.

Words such as 'sent down' are a symbolic way of indicating that His message is from God and is not the product of human intellect. Such terminology is understood in Bahá'í interpretation to be unrelated to any physical place.[23] Since God is omnipresent (Ps. 139:7–10), omnipotent (Rev. 19:6) and omniscient (Isa. 46:10), God's reality transcends the distances and limitations of the material world. Therefore, such expressions in the Scriptures as 'sent down' are intended to convey symbolically a divine significance which could not otherwise be expressed,[24] and do not refer to a geographic location.

This expression, 'sent down', is also parallel to words of Jesus, who stated, 'I have come down from heaven'

---

22. The title 'Object of the adoration of the world' expresses conceptually what was translated more literally in the earlier version as the 'Kibla of the world'. The original Arabic word 'Kibla' (sometimes spelled 'Qiblah'), refers to the direction and point to which Muslims face when offering their daily prayers. The direction and point of the Kibla, in Islam, is the Ka'ba (i.e. the House of God), the central shrine of Islam, specifically the cube-like building which stands at the centre of the great open-air Mosque of Mecca. The Ka'ba is also the central place of pilgrimage for Muslims. As the centre of Islamic worship the Ka'ba can be said to be parallel in significance to the Tabernacle in ancient Israelite practice. Around AD 624 Muhammad instructed Muslims to face the Ka'ba (Qur'án 2:142–5) instead of Jerusalem when praying. This symbolized the break between Islamic practice and the religious practices of the past, a break much like that of Christianity from certain Jewish traditions and practices. Bahá'u'lláh's use of the term 'Kibla' in connection with Himself, suggests that the Temple or House of God is now represented by Him. As instructed by Bahá'u'lláh, Bahá'ís regard the Shrine of Bahá'u'lláh, in 'Akká, Israel, as the Ka'ba for this age. By identifying Himself as the 'Object of the adoration of the world' or 'Kibla', Bahá'u'lláh has clearly set out the exalted nature of His claim – to be the One empowered and appointed by God to inaugurate a new Covenant at this point in the history of the world.
23. 'Abdu'l-Bahá, SAQ, ch. 23.
24. Ibid., ch. 16.

(John 6:38)[25] and 'the Father who sent Me' (John 12:49). So, when Bahá'u'lláh says that this tablet has been 'sent down from the holy kingdom', He is making a claim like that of Christ, that is, He is asserting that His words have divine authority. Similarly, by characterizing Himself as 'He Who has come from the heaven of eternity', Bahá'u'lláh conveys that His own life and mission are established by the will of God (KI 66). With these words it becomes clear that His claim to divinity pertains not only to His words but also to His life.

The phrase 'heaven of eternity' expresses that state of being that is associated with divinity, or God: that which is beyond place or time, wholly above the nature humankind is subjected to in this contingent world. The reality of God is eternal whereas the reality of the world is ever-changing and subject to decay and death. By emphasizing that He has come from the heaven of eternity, Bahá'u'lláh stresses the divine and spiritual significance of His mission.

'Heaven' expresses the exalted or transcendent nature of God's Revelation. This truth can be seen in the words of the Bible. God is 'the High and Lofty One Who inhabits eternity', who dwells 'in the high and holy place' (Isa. 57:15) and whose 'throne is in heaven' (Ps. 11:4). Such verses use symbols which sound very material, but the immaterial nature of God was beautifully expressed and affirmed by Solomon in this verse, 'But will God indeed dwell on the earth? Behold, heaven and the heaven of heavens cannot contain You' (1 Kgs. 8:27). Solomon's words demonstrate that God's reality is not bound by physical limitations. Phrases such as the 'throne is in heaven' are not literal but symbolize God's sovereignty. Thus references to 'throne', like 'heaven', are appropriate symbols intended to express a condition or truth which we are unable otherwise to comprehend or convey pre-

---

25. All references to and quotations from the Holy Bible will utilize the New King James Version (NKJV) unless otherwise specified (see Bibliography for details).

cisely. It naturally follows that, in as much as 'heaven' is not the space surrounding the globe, Bahá'u'lláh's use of such expressions as 'sent down', are not intended literally. Heaven is a spiritual reality, and words such as 'sent down' are meant to convey a relationship to that reality.

By stating that He is 'invested with transcendent glory' Bahá'u'lláh further emphasizes that His mission is authorized not by human powers but by divine authority. The words 'invested with transcendent glory' point out that His glory is spiritual and thus, unlike the things that the world glories in, it is a glory that is divine in nature and will not pass away. The word 'glory' also appears in the invocation, 'In the name of the Lord, the Lord of great glory'. The true significance of glory and its relationship to Bahá'u'lláh is a theme which continues throughout this tablet and has a very special importance with regard to Bible prophecies. This will be explained more thoroughly later.

All these points affirm the Messianic nature of Bahá'u'lláh's claims. The fuller nature of these claims, as well as a defence of them, unfolds as this tablet progresses.

II

1 This is an Epistle from Our presence unto him whom the veils of names have failed to keep back from God, the Creator of earth and heaven, that his eyes may be cheered in the days of his Lord, the Help in Peril, the Self-Subsisting.

COMMENTARY

This tablet is given as an inspiration to one who has not allowed obstacles and doubts to prevent him from acknowledging Bahá'u'lláh's claims. Although it appears to have been written in honour of one person, the one whom 'the veils of names have failed to keep back from God', its contents are addressed to all people and to Christians specifically. This will become more evident as we examine more of the tablet. It should also be noted that while many of Bahá'u'lláh's tablets are addressed to individual recipients, Bahá'u'lláh clearly states that they are intended for wider audiences. He writes:

> The summons and the message which We gave were never intended to reach or to benefit one land or one people only. Mankind in its entirety must firmly adhere to whatsoever hath been revealed and vouchsafed unto it. Then and only then will it attain unto true liberty. The whole earth is illuminated with the resplendent glory of God's Revelation (TB 89).

Bahá'u'lláh indicates that the reason this tablet was written in honour of this individual who has recognized Him, is so that 'his eyes may be cheered'. In other words, it is intended to bring the recipient happiness and comfort. And for any believer such an honour would, no doubt, be an unimaginably great blessing. But, in addition, the message itself imparts the blessings of its spiritual guidance.

In this same verse, Bahá'u'lláh refers to Himself as this person's 'Lord'. From the Bahá'í point of view, Bahá'u'lláh represents, like all Prophets or Manifestations of God, God's eternal lordship in the spiritual sovereignty He possesses. Bahá'u'lláh adds to the title 'Lord' the descriptive attributes 'the Help in Peril, the Self-Subsisting'. These attributes convey the idea that, as One appointed to mediate on behalf of God, Bahá'u'lláh is the One to whom the believer can turn for assistance and guidance. By placing these two attributes together the text conveys the central religious truth that God, who is in need of no one (Self-Subsisting), helps those who are in need (i.e. Peril). Moreover, this help is not confined simply to assistance in times of material crisis; rather, it is a necessary spiritual assistance, owing to the station of humankind in relation to God.

The inherent qualities of the human station can be looked at in a number of ways. But, for the purpose of this commentary, they can simply be summarized, on the one hand, as humankind's need to attain salvation and, on the other hand, as the inescapable limitations which prevent people from attaining that salvation without God's help. Hence God provides this help, as all the sacred Scriptures abundantly testify.

III

1 Say, O followers of the Son!

COMMENTARY

The phrase 'followers of the Son' is an all-inclusive way of referring to the followers of Jesus Christ, since they do not all refer to themselves directly as Christians, some for instance, calling themselves Roman Catholics, Anglicans, Presbyterians, Baptists, and so on. This paragraph shows that, while this tablet may have been written in honour of one person, its message is intended for a wide audience, especially Christians. It marks the beginning of the tablet's call to them. The first verses of this call are also the beginning of a defence by Bahá'u'lláh of His Faith.

2 Have ye shut out yourselves from Me by reason of My Name?
3 Wherefore ponder ye not in your hearts?
4 Day and night ye have been calling upon your Lord, the Omnipotent, but when He came from the heaven of eternity in His great glory, ye turned aside from Him and remained sunk in heedlessness.

COMMENTARY

Bahá'u'lláh begins His address to Christians by asking why they hesitate to embrace His Faith. He asks: Is it because of His name? The significance of addressing this particular objection may be that Bahá'u'lláh wishes to prevent Christians from becoming preoccupied with superficial judgements which are not related to the discernment of His actual spiritual station.

The name or title of a Messenger of God is an outward expression of His spiritual reality. This is evident once it is understood that, for example, the name 'Christ' is the Greek word for 'Messiah', meaning 'the Anointed', which is intended to convey the divinely appointed station of Jesus (Ps. 105:15, Isa. 45:1).[26] Jesus acknowledges His claim to be appointed by God and the expected Messiah when He reads from the book of Isaiah in the synagogue:

> The Spirit of the LORD is upon Me, *because He has anointed Me* to preach the gospel to the poor. He has sent Me to heal the brokenhearted, to preach deliverance to the captives and recovery of sight to the blind, to set at liberty those who are oppressed, to preach the acceptable year of the Lord. (Luke 4:18–19, emphasis added; see also Isa. 61:1,2; Acts 10:38).

When Jesus stated that God had 'anointed' Him, He was claiming to be the Christ. To have been anointed meant that God had given Him authority. This concept is derived from ancient times when ritual anointing was performed on kings as a sign that God had chosen them for or appointed them to their positions of authority.[27]

In the same way that Jesus Christ is a name or title meaning 'Jesus is anointed of God', Bahá'u'lláh is an Arabic name or title which, translated, means 'the Glory

---

26. The name Christ is the English form of the Greek verbal adjective 'Christos' used to translate the Hebrew equivalent meaning 'anointed'.
27. See *New Bible Dictionary*, 2nd edn, p. 50.

of God'. Reference to 'the glory of God' begins in the Old Testament and appears with strong Messianic character in such passages as, 'And behold, the glory of the God of Israel came from the way of the east. His voice was like the sound of many waters; and the earth shone with His glory' (Ezek. 43:2). In the Gospel, the revelation of God's glory is clearly associated with the second coming of Christ by references to 'the Son of Man' who 'comes in the glory of His Father' (e.g. Mark 8:38, 13:26).

There are many passages in the Bible containing the phrase 'the glory of God', or a variation of it. Bahá'í writings assert that some of these are references to Bahá'u'lláh, such as the prophetic passage, 'And the city had no need of the sun or of the moon to shine in it, for the glory of God illumined it, and the Lamb is its light' (Rev. 21:23).[28] This verse correlates 'the glory of God' in a Messianic context with the 'Lamb' which is a symbol for Jesus Christ (John 1:29, 36). Some other examples are: 'The glory of the LORD shall be revealed, and all flesh shall see it together; for the mouth of the LORD has spoken' (Isa. 40:5), and 'The excellence of Carmel and Sharon.[29] They shall see the glory of the LORD, the excellency of our God' (Isa. 35:2).[30]

The concept of the glory of God denotes the revelation of God's spiritual presence, nature, and attributes.[31] Later, as the following commentaries unfold, the significance of Bahá'u'lláh's name will become increasingly evident as we examine the spiritual nature of His glory.

There are several other possible reasons why Bahá'u'lláh asks Christians if they object to Him because of His name. First, some Christians may object to the name Bahá'u'lláh because it is commonly believed that Christ

28. Shoghi Effendi, *GPB*, pp. 94–5.
29. Carmel is Hebrew for 'garden-land' or 'fruitful land' and the name of a range of hills in Israel which is associated with Elijah. Bahá'u'lláh visited Mount Carmel, and today this is the site of the Bahá'í World Centre. Sharon means a level place or plain and is the name of the coastal plains of north Israel which can be seen looking south from Mount Carmel.
30. Shoghi Effendi, *GPB*, p. 94.
31. See *New Bible Dictionary*, 2nd edn, pp. 423–4.

will return with the same name. The New Testament itself states, 'Jesus Christ is the same yesterday, today, and forever' (Heb. 13:8). Also, the Apostle Peter declared, 'there is no other name under heaven given among men by which we must be saved' (Acts 4:12).

Christian scholars have raised a number of points that should be considered with regard to this issue. For instance, as some Christian commentators have noted, it does not seem reasonable that Peter intends by 'no other name' only the Greek words 'Jesus Christ'. They assert that another 'name' of Jesus is 'the Word of God' (Rev. 19:13), which suggests much wider possibilities.[32] In Peter's day, Jesus's name had a special significance which was evident to those who heard it, and it was this meaning or reality of Christ that he intended when he said, 'no other name'. The reality of Christ is synonymous with His divine authority and 'the Word of God'.

Furthermore, there are many verses in the Bible that suggest the Scriptures do not insist on the name Jesus Christ exclusively. For example, Isaiah refers to the future Messiah with these words, 'And His name will be called Wonderful, Counsellor, Mighty God, Everlasting Father, Prince of Peace' (Isa. 9:6). Isaiah makes no mention of the name 'Jesus Christ'.[33] And, in another passage, Isaiah prophesied that His name would be Immanuel (Isa. 7:14). We know this prophecy is applicable to Christ's first advent because it is recorded as fulfilled in the Gospel of Matthew (1:23). In as much as Jesus is generally not referred to as Immanuel, Christians acknowledge that the truth and fulfilment of this prophecy involves the significance of the name which, when translated, means 'God with us'. Similarly, we can ask: is it not appropriate and equally true to refer to Christ as 'the Glory of God'?

---

32. E. C. Dewick, *The Christian Attitude to Other Religions*, p. 92. Also Geoffrey Parrinder, *Avatar and Incarnation*, p. 270.

33. These points should not be construed as a demotion of the greatness of Christ or His name. The Bahá'í writings consistently glorify the reality of Christ and all the Prophets. 'Abdu'l-Bahá is reported to have said, 'His [Jesus's] name is eternal and His glory everlasting' (*PUP* p. 210; see also pp. 282, 395).

In addition to these passages there are indications in the Book of Revelation that Jesus and His followers will, in fact, use a different name. Even some Christian scholars have pointed this out, citing this passage, 'He who overcomes, I will make him a pillar in the temple of My God, and he shall go out no more. And I will write on him the name of My God and the name of the city of My God, the new Jerusalem, which comes down out of heaven from My God: And I will write on him My new name' (Rev. 3:12).[34] Some commentators believe the new name referred to is indicated in Revelation 19:13 or 19:16, but other Christian scholars disagree, citing this verse, 'And I will give him a white stone, and on the stone a new name written which no one knows except him who receives it' (Rev. 2:17).[35]

Bahá'u'lláh further identifies Himself as the fulfilment of New Testament prophecy in the following passages. After Bahá'u'lláh asks: 'Have ye shut out yourselves from Me by reason of My Name?' He continues with these words, 'Wherefore ponder ye not in your hearts? Day and night[36] ye have been calling upon your Lord, the Omnipotent, but when He came from the heaven of eternity in His great glory, ye turned aside from Him and remained sunk in heedlessness.' In stating that He has come 'from the heaven of eternity in His great glory', Bahá'u'lláh

---

34. Shoghi Effendi identifies this passage with Bahá'u'lláh's Revelation. See *LG*, p. 41.
35. For Christian scholars who believe Christ will return with a new name, see I. T. Beckwith, *The Apocalypse of John*, p. 468, John Lange, *Commentary on the Holy Scriptures*, vol. 12 (see Rev. 19:16), or R. C. Trench, *Commentary on the Epistles to the Seven Churches in Asia*, pp. 198–9. The expectation of a new name is also found in popular Christian literature. Billy Graham writes, 'We have the glorious promise to him that overcometh, "a new name"' (*Approaching Hoofbeats*, pp. 43, 51).
36. The words 'day and night' could have two meanings. They could have the conventional sense of a 24-hour period of time or they could metaphorically represent the daytime and the night-time of the religion of Christ. The word 'day' symbolizes the early time of Christianity when the light of Christ, so to speak, was bright (John 9:5). Night symbolizes the decline of Christianity, a time of spiritual darkness when conflicts and disagreements divide the Church, and people depart from the teachings of Christ (*KI* p. 31).

indicates that His appearance is the fulfilment of Jesus's prophecy that 'the Son of Man' will come 'on the clouds of heaven with power and great glory' (Matt. 24:30). The following comments will be concerned with His appearance in the 'clouds of heaven'. Bahá'u'lláh's appearance in 'power and great glory' will be discussed later in the commentaries on verses VI:2 and XVIII:5.

Many Christians have believed for centuries that this verse, and others like it, refer to the visible heavens, that is, the actual sky and space above the material earth. As we have already said, Bahá'í writings explain that the 'heaven' Christ spoke of is not a physical location, but refers to a spiritual reality. 'Abdu'l-Bahá writes, explaining 'clouds' in connection with 'heaven' and Jesus's return:

> Verily the heaven into which the Messiah rose up was not this unending sky, rather was His heaven the Kingdom of His beneficent Lord. Even as He Himself hath said, 'I came down from heaven' [John 6:38], and again, 'The Son of Man is in heaven' [John 3:13]. Hence it is clear that His heaven is beyond all directional points; it encircleth all existence, and is raised up for those who worship God. Beg and implore thy Lord to lift thee up into that heaven, and give thee to eat of its food, in this age. (SWA 167).

'Abdu'l-Bahá continues, 'Know thou that the people, even unto this day, have failed to unravel the hidden secrets of the Book [Bible]'. He points out that Christ was always in heaven, and that His descent from heaven and resurrection symbolize important spiritual truths. Using common scientific knowledge of the sky and clouds, 'Abdu'l-Bahá explains the improbability of a literal interpretation of the Scriptures. He then writes: 'Rather, the cloud referred to in the Gospel is the human body, so called because the body is as a veil to man, which, even as a cloud, preventeth him from beholding the Sun of Truth that shineth from the horizon of Christ' (SWA 167–8).

This suggests that it is possible to see or know about the visible return of Christ but not to recognize Him because of the clouds of our doubts and misunderstandings. This will be discussed further in the commentary on verse VII:7.

In this tablet, Bahá'u'lláh Himself does not engage in a lengthy explanation about His name or His appearance in the 'clouds of heaven'. Instead, He chooses to compel Christians to reconsider their objections to Him by reminding them of those who objected to Christ. This is the main point of the next paragraph.

IV

1 Consider those who rejected the Spirit[37] when He came unto them with manifest dominion.

COMMENTARY

Bahá'u'lláh begins this tablet by asking the Christians about their objections to Him. Then, as a warning, He calls attention to the objections of those who rejected Christ.

In the Gospel it is recorded that many people, most notably the Pharisees[38] or religious leaders, rejected the claims of Christ. This happened, Bahá'u'lláh says, even though Christ came with 'manifest dominion'. Naturally, this raises the questions: if the sovereignty of Christ was apparent, why did the people who were the recognized religious leaders of their day reject Him? Where was the dominion of Christ?

---

37. The word or title 'Spirit' is frequently used by Bahá'u'lláh to refer to Jesus Christ. This title and the title 'Spirit of God', which is found in sayings attributed to Muḥammad (see Parrinder, *Jesus in the Qur'án*, pp. 48–51), may be intended to convey the divine nature and relationship of Jesus to God. Paul uses the word Spirit to refer to Christ and God (Rom. 8:9).

38. The Pharisees were a Jewish faction opposed to the priestly aristocracy (the Sadducees). Although a minority group, they were the group most representative of the beliefs of the Jewish people and held a dominant influence in the Jewish governing body, the Sanhedrin. They were also characterized by strong eschatological expectations. (*New Bible Dictionary*, pp. 924–5, and *The Encyclopedia of Religion*, p. 580).

To have dominion means to rule or to have power to rule, to have sovereignty. In many of His writings, Bahá'u'lláh emphasizes that real sovereignty and dominion are not of this world but are, rather, spiritual and eternal (KI 105–11). In the Kitáb-i-Íqán, Bahá'u'lláh illustrates this point by referring to the example of Jesus:

> It is also recorded in the Gospel according to St. Luke, that on a certain day Jesus passed by a Jew sick of the palsy, and lay upon a couch. When the Jew saw Him, he recognized Him, and cried out for His help. Jesus said unto him: 'Arise from thy bed; thy sins are forgiven thee.' Certain of the Jews, standing by, protested saying: 'Who can forgive sins, but God alone?' And immediately He perceived their thoughts, Jesus answering said unto them: 'Whether is it easier, to say to the sick of the palsy, arise, and take up thy bed, and walk; or to say, thy sins are forgiven thee? that ye may know that the Son of Man hath power on earth to forgive sins.' This is the real sovereignty, and such is the power of God's chosen Ones! (KI 133–4; see also Luke 5:18–25, Mark 2:3–12).

There is an argument, which appears frequently in Bahá'í writings demonstrating the spiritual nature of Jesus's sovereignty, which goes somewhat as follows: the Jews expected the Messiah to come as a ruler (Matt. 2:3–6 and John 12:12–13), with a throne (Isa. 9:6–7) and sword (Isa. 66:16) as prophesied. They expected the Messiah to liberate them from their subjugation by the Roman government.[39] In so far as the Pharisees could see, since Jesus was not a ruler and He had no sword or throne, in their judgement He was not the Messiah. Moreover Christ

---

39. 'The Jews of Palestine, who had fondly expected a temporal deliverer, gave so cold a reception to the miracles of the divine prophet, that it was found unnecessary to publish, or at least to preserve, any Hebrew gospel' (Edward Gibbon, The Decline and Fall of the Roman Empire, p. 182).

made claims which, in their understanding, were blasphemous and deserved the death penalty (Matt. 26:63–7). However, if we look at the example of those who acknowledged the claims of Jesus, particularly the Apostles, we find that, for them, it was apparent that Jesus was indeed a ruler. This is evident in the fact that they perceived Him as Lord, even to the extent that Peter said, 'He is Lord of all' (Acts 10:36). He had fulfilled the prophecies, but in a spiritual way. He had come as a King (John 18:37), His sword was His teachings (Matt. 10:34, Eph. 6:17, 2 Cor. 10:3–5), and He was given the throne of David (Luke 1:32, Acts 7:49). Jesus had come 'to preach deliverance to the captives' (Luke 4:18), not as One who was to liberate them from Rome as they had hoped, but as One who came to liberate people from sin. Jesus did not come to be ruler of this temporal world (John 18:36), but rather came as one who was already the eternal ruler of that Kingdom of God that is within us (Luke 17:20–1).[40]

Bahá'u'lláh begins by raising the issue of Christian objections to His Faith, and then refers to the Gospel for historical examples to counter those objections. It seems clear that Bahá'u'lláh intends to provoke the Christians who object to Him to ask themselves how these objections differ from the objections of those who opposed Christ. If they had lived at the time of Christ and expected a deliverer as the Jews expected, would they have accepted Christ or would they have disputed with Him? At that time, were the dominion and the spiritual evidences of Christ any more apparent than those of Bahá'u'lláh today? In the next verse, Bahá'u'lláh points out that the Pharisees rejected Christ even though they had fervently hoped for and awaited His appearance.

---

40. Discourses on Jesus's fulfilment of prophecy can be found in 'Abdu'l-Bahá, *PT*, pp. 54–7 and *SWA*, pp. 44–6.

2 How numerous the Pharisees who had secluded themselves in synagogues in His name, lamenting over their separation from Him, and yet when the portals of reunion were flung open and the divine Luminary shone resplendent from the Dayspring of Beauty, they disbelieved in God, the Exalted, the Mighty.

COMMENTARY

According to the Gospel, the chief priests and the Pharisees had long expected and hoped for the appearance of Christ (Matt. 2:4), yet when He did appear they rejected Him:

> Then the officers came to the chief priests and Pharisees, who said to them, 'Why have you not brought Him [Jesus]?' The officers answered, 'No man ever spoke like this Man!' Then the Pharisees answered them, 'Are you also deceived? Have any of the rulers or the Pharisees believed in Him? But this crowd that does not know the law is accursed' (John 7:45–9).

Bahá'u'lláh charges that the Pharisees, by rejecting Christ, in effect also 'disbelieved in God'. The truth of this is suggested by many statements made by Christ Himself, such as, 'He who does not honour the Son does not honour the Father who sent Him' (John 5:23), and 'You know neither Me nor My Father. If you had known Me, you would have known My Father also' (John 8:19; see also 14:7). Bahá'u'lláh teaches that it is only through the Manifestations of God – God's Prophets and Messengers – that humankind can come to know God (GWB 66–7), even as Jesus points out with particular regard to Himself, 'I am the way, the truth, and the life. No one comes to the Father except through Me' (John 14:6).

Bahá'u'lláh first points out that Christ appeared 'with

manifest dominion'. Then He asserts that the rejection of Christ was essentially a rejection of God. Both these points stress that, from Bahá'u'lláh's point of view, there were clear spiritual signs in Christ which testified that He was sent by God. God was manifest in Christ Himself by His many divine virtues and attributes, and His dominion was manifest in the spiritual transformation He effected in those who believed in Him. In the next verse Bahá'u'lláh adds to this spiritual evidence, manifest in Christ Himself, the evidence of Old Testament prophecies that testified to Christ.

3 They failed to attain His presence, notwithstanding that His advent had been promised them in the Book of Isaiah as well as in the Books of the Prophets and the Messengers.

COMMENTARY

Here, Bahá'u'lláh points out that the people who were most learned in the Scriptures failed to acknowledge Christ despite the numerous prophecies foretelling His coming. They had studied the Bible, read the prophecies, fully expected His coming, and yet failed to acknowledge Him. It seems reasonable to assume that Bahá'u'lláh is suggesting that it is unwise to rely too much on contemporary interpretations of Scripture and unwise, as well, to leave decisions of faith to religious leaders.

Prophecies will perhaps always remain an area of dispute. Both the interpretation of prophecy and the degree to which a fulfilled prophecy substantiates Messianic claims are debatable. However, from a biblical point of view, Bahá'u'lláh's assertion is supported by an ample listing of prophecies in the four Gospels which relate to the events and claims associated with the appearance of Jesus Christ.

We might ask, how convincing are those prophecies? Should they have been considered a sufficient sign to the Pharisees? Are the prophecies cited in Bahá'í texts equal in testimony?

4   No one from among them turned his face towards the Dayspring of divine bounty[41] except such as were destitute of any power amongst men.
5   And yet, today, every man endowed with power and invested with sovereignty prideth himself on His Name.

COMMENTARY

When Jesus appeared, almost everyone who had knowledge of the Scriptures and who possessed a position of power rejected Him. Those who accepted Him were generally without any substantial status in society. It seems reasonable that the opposite should have been true. Those who should have been the most likely to accept Him were those who knew the Scriptures. And then these people who knew the Scriptures and who had accepted Christ should have gone out to recruit and educate the destitute and the less informed. Just as today, who expects to be the first to accept Christ when He returns but the Christians who have studied the Scriptures and eagerly await His appearance? By pointing out how the Pharisees rejected Christ, Bahá'u'lláh demonstrates to Christians that, while it seems unlikely to them that they could make such an error, it neverthe-

---

41. 'Dayspring' refers to Christ and probably expresses the nature of His appearance, the Daybreak of God's light (revelation) in that time (the Day of the Lord, signifying a time of Judgement, John 3:19); 'of divine bounty' indicates that the appearance of Christ is a manifestation of God's kindness, a sign of God's love for humankind. 'Through the tender mercy of God, with which the Dayspring from on high has visited us' (Luke 1:78, see also Qur'án 19:21).

less happened to the Pharisees and could happen to them too.

Bahá'u'lláh adamantly rejects the belief that one must be learned or trained as a priest to comprehend the Scriptures. He points out that one does not need such credentials to be able to recognize God's Manifestations or understand the Scriptures. He states that the assertion that common people can 'neither grasp their meaning nor appreciate their value' is 'utterly fallacious and inadmissible', actuated by 'arrogance and pride', and motivated by individuals attempting 'to tighten the reins of their authority over the people.'[42] He continues:

> In the sight of God, these common people are infinitely superior and exalted above their religious leaders who have turned away from the one true God. The understanding of His words and the comprehension of the utterances of the Birds of Heaven are in no wise dependent upon human learning. They depend solely upon purity of heart, chastity of soul, and freedom of spirit (KI 210–11).

In the Gospel the Apostles Peter, Andrew, James and John were only fishermen (Matt. 4:18, Luke 5:1–10, Mark 1:19–20).[43] Matthew is recorded as having worked as a

---

42. There is evidence that in early Christian times, Bible reading was common among the laity. However, 'With the collapse of the ancient civilization and the decay of learning, the following centuries, naturally enough, brought a decline in the reading of the Bible ... laymen could not read, and when they had again learned the art they were not allowed to read the Bible. This was part of the mediaeval system of keeping the laity in dependence upon ecclesiastical authority, and was based upon the idea of the unfathomableness of the mysteries which the Scripture contained. The traditional exegesis of the Church was the only means of reaching these, and the laity, left to themselves, always wandered from the track.' This attitude was still apparent during the nineteenth century. Bible societies attempting to put the Bible in the hands of the common person were suppressed. 'Leo XII published an encyclical against them in 1824, and Pius IX, in the syllabus of 1864, condemned them along with Socialism, Communism, and Secret Societies.' See the entry for Bible In the Church, VI, *Encyclopedia of Religion and Ethics*, vol. II, pp. 607–8.

43. 'Our serious thoughts will suggest to us that the apostles themselves were chosen by Providence among the fishermen of Galilee, and that, the lower we depress the temporal condition of the first Christians, the more reason we

tax collector for the Romans (Luke 5:27). Jesus Himself stated, 'I thank you, Father, Lord of heaven and earth, because you have hidden these things from the wise and prudent and have revealed them to babes' (Matt. 11:25). Had these individuals gone to the learned priests to ask about the truth of Christ and had they accepted their verdicts, all of history would have been changed.

The people who occupied positions of authority in government and religion not only failed to acknowledge Christ but openly opposed Him (John 18:12–14). This is, of course, no discredit to Jesus but, rather, an indication that those who boast knowledge as well as temporal power are often blinded by pride, too attached to their own points of view, and more concerned with perpetuating their careers than with investigating and affirming the truth (KI 14–15, 164–5).

In other writings Bahá'u'lláh points out that such leaders of religion have not only frequently failed to acknowledge such Manifestations of God as Christ, but have also prevented others from doing so. Bahá'u'lláh writes: 'The leaders of religion, in every age, have hindered their people from attaining the shores of eternal salvation, inasmuch as they held the reins of authority in their mighty grasp' (KI 15). For this reason He repeatedly emphasized that 'man can never hope to attain unto the knowledge of the All-Glorious ... unless and until he ceases to regard the words and deeds of mortal men as a standard for the true understanding and recognition of God and His Prophets' (KI 3–4).

In verse IV:5, Bahá'u'lláh points out that, in contrast to the early years of the mission of Jesus, Christianity has now gained recognition among people in positions of

---

shall find to admire their merit and success. It is incumbent on us diligently to remember that the kingdom of heaven was promised to the poor in spirit, and that minds afflicted by calamity and the contempt of mankind cheerfully listen to the divine promise of future happiness; while, on the contrary, the fortunate are satisfied with the possession of this world; and the wise abuse in doubt and dispute their vain superiority of reason and knowledge' (Gibbon, *The Decline and Fall of the Roman Empire*, p. 189).

power, who take pride in being called 'Christian'. While still true today, this was even more the case at the time Bahá'u'lláh wrote this tablet. In the late 1800s a handful of European countries, regarding themselves as 'Christian nations', were busily colonizing virtually the entire planet.[44] This transition from rejection to acceptance among people of authority suggests the error of the Pharisees as well as the power and influence of Christ, which triumphed despite the fact that He was initially thought to be an imposter. This also suggests a parallel with Bahá'u'lláh.

6 Moreover, call thou to mind the one who sentenced Jesus to death.
7 He was the most learned of His age in His own country, whilst he who was only a fisherman believed in Him.
8 Take good heed and be of them that observe the warning.

COMMENTARY

The failure of a learned person to recognize a prophet is nowhere more clearly demonstrated in the Bible than in

---

44. 'To a greater or lesser degree all the European nations felt the same consciousness of destiny and duty to others. The degree of sympathy, of Christian humanitarianism, developed by the West for the whole of mankind, undoubtedly influenced its colonial development. Most French action in Indo-China, for instance, cannot be understood unless the significance of the Christian missionary movement in French colonial history is appreciated. It did not play a minor but a major role in determining French policy. There is a great deal of recent world history which cannot be understood without taking account of the Christian missions. With the benefit of hindsight it is not difficult to see that the ethics and the political ideology of the West would eventually be rejected by Africans and Asians. But the West was not to know this in the nineteenth century. Nor is it difficult to show how the "missionary urge" and the "civilizing mission" were often used to cloak less worthy aims' (William Woodruff, *Impact of Western Man*, pp. 45–54).

the example of Caiaphas, the high priest. And it is likely that this is who Bahá'u'lláh refers to as 'the most learned of His [Christ's] age'. It was Caiaphas[45] (Matt. 25:57), who advised the Jews that Jesus should be killed (John 18:14). In the Gospel of Matthew the trial is recorded as follows,

> Jesus kept silent. And the high priest answered and said to Him, 'I adjure You by the living God that You tell us if You are the Christ, the Son of God.' Jesus said to him, 'It is as you said. Nevertheless, I say to you, hereafter you will see the Son of Man sitting at the right hand of the Power, and coming on the clouds of heaven.' Then the high priest tore his clothes, saying, 'He has spoken blasphemy! What further need do we have of witnesses? Look, now you have heard His blasphemy! What do you think?' They answered and said, 'He is deserving of death' (Matt. 26:63–6).

In contrast to the learned Caiaphas, there was Peter, who was only a fisherman (Matt. 4:10), untrained in the law, that is, in the Books of Moses (Acts 4:13). He was the first to acknowledge that Jesus was 'the Christ, the Son of the living God' (Matt. 16:16). By pointing out the failure of Caiaphas and the recognition that the less knowledgeable Peter accorded Christ, Bahá'u'lláh no doubt wishes to inspire some degree of humility in Christians who judge His claims. This understanding gives emphasis to the

---

45. Some argue that responsibility for the death of Christ rests with the Roman, Pontius Pilate. He was commander of the Roman army which occupied Israel at the time of Christ. Because the capital sentences of the Sanhedrin had to be submitted to him for his ratification, blame is sometimes attributed to him for Jesus's death. It has been argued that the Romans were trying to prevent another uprising. However, the Jews were responsible, according to the Gospels, for bringing the matter before Pilate. The Bahá'í writings consistently put the responsibility with the Jewish leaders of that time. It is also improbable that Bahá'u'lláh intends Pilate, since He says he 'was the most learned' of Christ's age. Caiaphas was high priest from AD 18 to 36. *New Bible Dictionary*, pp. 157, 939–40. See also Abbe Eban, *Heritage: Civilization and the Jews*, pp. 106, 118.

admonition to 'take good heed and be of them that observe the warning'.

In this paragraph Bahá'u'lláh shows that the Jews expected Christ, that Christ appeared with divine virtues which testified to His truth, that Christ transformed those who accepted Him, that He fulfilled the prophecies of Scripture, and yet the most learned of the Jews rejected and opposed Him. In the next paragraph, Bahá'u'lláh draws a parallel between these events and the reception accorded to His Faith.

V

1 Consider likewise, how numerous at this time are the monks who have secluded themselves in their churches, calling upon the Spirit, but when He appeared through the power of Truth, they failed to draw nigh unto Him and are numbered with those that have gone far astray.
2 Happy are they that have abandoned them and set their faces towards Him Who is the Desire of all that are in the heavens and all that are on the earth.

COMMENTARY

Bahá'u'lláh compares here the Christian monks of His day to the Pharisees who rejected Christ. He points out the fervent Messianic expectation of His (and our) time, when He states that the monks have secluded themselves in their churches, 'calling upon the Spirit'.[46] Notwithstanding this belief in Christ's return and their knowledge of the Scriptures, they did not discover and accept Bahá'u'lláh. In this way they 'are numbered with those that have gone far astray'. This assertion is probably not intended in a narrow way but, rather, suggests the in-

---

46. The 'Spirit' refers to Christ, but in this context, although the monks are calling on Christ, Bahá'u'lláh means this to be none other than Himself.

ability of the monks to recognize His Revelation despite having made a vocation of studying the Scriptures. Bahá'u'lláh therefore states that people should abandon the monks (perhaps meaning their outlook and practices).[47]

Bahá'u'lláh may have chosen to draw a parallel between the monks and the Pharisees because, of all categories of Christians, monks are perhaps most noted for their singular devotion to the religious life. The words 'monk' and 'monasticism' are derived from the Greek word meaning 'alone' or 'solitary', but monastic life does not involve absolute solitude. Monks live the religious life apart from the world but not apart from those who share the same principles of life.[48] Because of their devotion and the central role the Scriptures occupy in their lives, Bahá'u'lláh implies that they should have been among the first to embrace His Cause.

Verse V:2 contains the title 'Him Who is the Desire of all that are in the heavens and all that are on the earth.' Naturally, this title raises the question: How can Bahá'u'lláh be 'the Desire of all' when most of the world's people do not follow Him? First, it should be noted that while this title sounds all-inclusive, it may have a religious sense which is not as broad as it would suggest if taken literally.

Bahá'u'lláh uses two separate phrases in the title, 'in

---

47. Bahá'u'lláh does directly counsel the monks to change their practices, but this fact may not be specifically related to the above statement in the *Lawh-i-Aqdas* (V:2). 'The pious deeds of the monks and priests among the followers of the Spirit [Jesus] – upon Him be the peace of God – are remembered in His presence. In this Day, however, let them give up the life of seclusion and direct their steps towards the open world and busy themselves with that which will profit themselves and others. We have granted them leave to enter into wedlock that they may bring forth one who will make mention of God, the Lord of the seen and the unseen, the Lord of the Exalted Throne' (*TB* p. 24).

48. Monasticism grew out of an extreme view of renunciation and a literal interpretation of certain biblical verses, e.g. Matt. 5:3, 6:24, 19:12, 21. Paul's words were also influential in the justification of monastic practice (1 Cor. 7:7, 32–5) even though Paul prefaced his views on marriage with the understanding that on this subject his view was a personal opinion (1 Cor. 7:25–6).

the heavens' and 'on the earth'. The meaning of these phrases may be suggested by explanations provided in His book, the Kitáb-i-Íqán. The phrase, 'all that are in the heavens' may refer to heavens of 'Revelation' (KI 68), and imply, therefore, all the followers of the different religions of the world. The word 'earth' in the phrase, 'all that are on the earth' may mean 'earth of understanding' (KI 48), and thus the phrase may encompass all those who are of understanding. From this point of view, Bahá'u'lláh is indicating that through God's Revelation, that is, the Revelation mediated through Him, the spiritual desires of the pious followers of every religion can be satisfied, and the deepest aspirations of the person of understanding can be fulfilled.

To understand why Bahá'u'lláh would take such a title for Himself, it is essential to consider this title in relation to His claim to be the promised Deliverer foretold in the Scriptures of all the world's religions. People throughout the world await a promised Messiah or Deliverer who will usher in a reign of justice.[49]

According to the Bahá'í understanding, it is possible to say that Bahá'u'lláh is 'the Desire of all', in a religious sense, because the Person all these different religions prophesy is actually the same promised Deliverer. Bahá'u'lláh writes: 'All the Divine Books and Scriptures have predicted and announced unto men the advent of the Most Great Revelation. None can adequately recount the verses recorded in the Books of former ages which forecast this supreme Bounty, this most mighty Bestowal' (GPB 100).

The title is similar to Haggai 2:7, which in the New King James version suggests the Messianic title 'the

---

49. Shoghi Effendi refers to prophecies from other religions that concern Bahá'u'lláh. See GPB pp. 93–100. Bahá'ís believe that God has sent Prophets and Messengers to all the peoples of the world to guide them at different times according to their particular needs. Bahá'ís refer to this concept as progressive revelation. See Bahá'u'lláh, GWB pp. 74–6, 78–81.

Desire of All Nations'.[50] (Bahá'u'lláh also uses this type of title with reference to Himself in verse XXIII:1.)

---

50. The Bahá'í writings assert that this title refers to Bahá'u'lláh (Shoghi Effendi, GPB p. 95). However, most modern scholars doubt that Haggai 2:7 is actually a Messianic reference to a single person. Those who are familiar with this debate may find Frank E. Gaebelein's comments of interest. 'The difficulty is as follows: The Hebrew for "desire" (chemdah) is singular, but the verb translated "shall come" is plural. Therefore, many Hebrew scholars have insisted that the meaning cannot be "the desire of all nations," but rather that it must be "the desire of all things" or "the precious things of all nations." It is these "precious things," they say, that are to be thought of as coming to Christ.' Gaebelein, however, notes a number of reasons which suggest that this view is not entirely certain. He adds, 'Moreover, in Hebrew an abstract noun is often used instead of a concrete; thus a reference to the Messiah is not automatically ruled out on the basis of language considerations. The use of a plural verb does not militate against the Messianic interpretation, for there are instances in which the verb agrees with the second of the two nouns.' See *Four Minor Prophets, Obadiah, Jonah, Habakkuk, and Haggai*, pp. 226–9.

VI

1 They read the Evangel and yet refuse to acknowledge the All-Glorious Lord, notwithstanding that He hath come through the potency of His exalted, His mighty and gracious dominion.

COMMENTARY

In this passage Bahá'u'lláh conveys the conviction that the Christian Scriptures bear witness to the truth of His claims. Because the monks read the Evangel (a word from Greek, meaning 'to announce', signifying the Gospel[51]) Bahá'u'lláh asserts that they should be able to acknowledge His Cause. The argument is that if one understands the earlier Scriptures and believes in them, one should be able to see that the same spiritual dominion recorded in the Gospel concerning Christ is now manifest in Bahá'u'lláh. The earlier Scriptures also record numerous prophecies which, if correctly understood, will enable the seeker to recognize their fulfilment. This is similar to

---

51. Gospel comes from the Anglo-Saxon, god-spell, meaning 'God's story', and is used to translate the Greek 'euangelion', the equivalent to the Hebrew word meaning 'good tidings' or 'glad tidings'. See Isa. 61:1 and Luke 4:18. Thus Evangel and Gospel are derived from the same source and have the same meaning (Alan Richardson, ed., *A Theological Word Book of the Bible*, p. 100). Bahá'u'lláh speaks of the Gospel as the Word of God in the *Kitáb-i-Íqán*. He explains that the City of God is 'none other than the Word of God revealed in every age and dispensation. In the days of Moses it was the Pentateuch; in the days of Jesus the Gospel' (*KI* p. 199).

Christ's assertion, 'For if you believed Moses, you would believe Me; for he wrote about Me' (John 5:46).[52]

There is ample historical evidence to suggest that when the Bahá'í Faith arose in the nineteenth century, many Christians believed, as Bahá'ís assert today, that biblical teachings pointed to the return of Christ at that time. There are also many prophecies which, Bahá'ís argue, correspond to events associated with Bahá'u'lláh's life.

The mid-nineteenth century may have been one of history's most fervent periods of Messianic expectation. Throughout the Christian world every major denomination preached the imminent return of Christ. In America, the Baptist Evangelist William Miller, sometimes credited with founding the Adventist movement, with the support of other preachers, asserted and convinced many that the Bible foretold that Christ would return in 1844.[53] That year in fact marked the beginning of the Bahá'í Era. Christians in Germany known as Templers gave up their homes and settled in Israel at the base of Mount Carmel to await the appearance of Christ.[54] It was to this area that Bahá'u'lláh was exiled, and today it is the location of the Bahá'í World Centre.

In the following verses Bahá'u'lláh shifts the emphasis from the historical parallel with the Bible to arguments that pertain directly to the testimony of His own mission.

2 We, verily, have come for your sakes, and have borne the misfortunes of the world for your salvation.

---

52. In the same way, Muḥammad asks the Christians to put aside their own judgements and rely on the guidance of the Gospel instead: 'Let the people of the Gospel judge by what God hath revealed therein. If any do fail to judge by [the light of] what God hath revealed, they are [no better than] those who rebel.' (Qur'án 5:47).

53. Daniel Cohen, *Waiting for the Apocalypse*, pp. 13–34. The most extensive documentation on this issue is probably LeRoy Edwin Froom's four-volume study, *The Prophetic Faith of Our Fathers*. 'Abdu'l-Bahá calculates from the Bible the date 1844 for the appearance of Christ's second coming. These calculations are very similar to those of William Miller and many other Christian interpreters in the nineteenth century. See *SAQ*, ch. 10.

54. David S. Ruhe, *Door of Hope*, pp. 189–93.

3 Flee ye the One Who hath sacrificed His life that ye may be quickened?

COMMENTARY

At the heart of Bahá'u'lláh's personal testimony is His own sacrifice. It is likely that He wants Christians to consider why He has willingly suffered persecution. He could have recanted His claims and teachings and avoided these difficulties.

'We', meaning Himself and all the Prophets, 'have come for your sakes', that is, for the benefit and redemption of the world. The Prophets bear 'the misfortunes of the world' for our 'salvation'. He asks, 'Flee ye the One', that is, Bahá'u'lláh, 'who hath sacrificed His life that ye may be quickened?' To sacrifice one's life does not necessitate being killed. In the case of Bahá'u'lláh, He sacrificed His life in that He gave up all the pursuits that one might normally seek and completely dedicated His life to God for the salvation of the world. He sacrificed His physical well-being, comfort and freedom, for instance, when He was imprisoned for His claims and teachings. His whole life was filled with such sacrifices because of the mission He accepted. The word 'quickened' means to bring to life or restore to life. In this context, it means to give spiritual life. Christ stated, 'It is the spirit that quickeneth'[55] the flesh profiteth nothing: the words that I speak unto you, they are spirit, and they are life' (KJV, John 6:63). The word of God is the source of spiritual life.

Bahá'u'lláh was born a nobleman in Persia in 1817 and could probably have enjoyed a long life of wealth and comfort as well as considerable renown in the government of the Sháh. It is possible He would have succeeded His father, Mírzá Buzurg, who held a position in the ministerial circle of the Sháh's government.[56] Instead,

---

55. NKJV reads, 'the Spirit Who gives life'. The translation of the NKJV reflects the doctrinal teaching of the spirit being a person, that is, the third person of the Holy Spirit in the Christian doctrine of the Trinity.
56. H. M. Balyuzi, *Bahá'u'lláh*, pp. 9–10; Shoghi Effendi, *GPB*, p. 94.

because He continued to advance His teachings, His temporal wealth was taken away from Him and He spent the rest of His life living as an exile under persecution and the threat of execution. Bahá'ís believe that it stands as a great testimony to Bahá'u'lláh's love and compassion that He suffered as He did to spiritually redeem a world which often showed indifference or open hostility to Him. Christ stated, 'Greater love has no one than this, than to lay down one's life for his friends' (John 15:13). It can be argued that Bahá'u'lláh laid down His life not only for His friends but for all humankind. In this degree of sacrifice one can see the divine love of God for humankind. In the writings of Paul we find, 'But God demonstrates His own love for us, in that while we were still sinners, Christ died for us' (Rom. 5:8).

Many times 'Abdu'l-Bahá stated that Bahá'u'lláh suffered, 'in order that a manifestation of selflessness and service might become apparent in the world of humanity; that the Most Great Peace should become a reality' (*PUP* 28). Peter also ascribes a similar purpose to Christ with these words, 'For Christ also suffered once for sins, the just for the unjust, that He might bring us to God' (1 Pet. 3:18). It is in relation to this aspect of His life that Bahá'u'lláh asks, why flee from One who has suffered so much for the betterment of others?

Among some Christians there is the general belief that the sacrifice made by Christ was essentially the last such sacrifice; when Jesus returns He will come with glory and power of a nature similar to that of temporal rulers, only superior to it, and that He will defeat the forces of evil. These Christians believe that after this battle Christ will establish His throne on earth.[57] Therefore many Christians

---

57. The opponents of the returned Christ are 'killed with the sword which proceeded from the mouth of Him who sat on the horse' (Rev. 19:21). Some Christians believe real armies will be led against Christ or those who are aligned with good, and that Christ will defeat His opponents with His word, not with military force. See Paul Lee Tan, *The Interpretation of Prophecy*, p. 347; John Wesley White, *Re-entry*, pp. 131–67. Hal Lindsey, in his popular book, *The Late Great Planet Earth*, asserts that Christ will use thermo-nuclear weapons (p. 175). Lindsey arrives at this conclusion by interpreting Zechariah 14:12.

do not expect Him to return and suffer again. The prophecies of Jesus in Matthew (ch. 24), Revelation (ch. 19) and the teachings concerning the sacrifice of Jesus in Hebrews (ch. 9) are some of the principal Scriptures which, through interpretation, form the basis of this Christian understanding.

The writings of the Bahá'í Faith find complete accord with these biblical passages when approached from a different perspective. The glory and power of Bahá'u'lláh are, in fact, revealed in His suffering, first, because the truth of His words and the spirituality of His life could not be overcome and destroyed by His persecutors. His power is therefore manifest in His invincibility and His glory is evident in His triumph over the persecution He suffered. Second, the triumph of His Cause and its spiritual transformation of the people who accept His teachings is another sign of His victory over the forces of opposition. His power and glory are not concerned with a temporal victory such as a military general seeks but are, rather, seen in His spiritual victory – His triumph despite the rejection and persecution He suffered. He does not come in the glory of men, but in 'the glory of the Father' (Mark 8:38).

The sacrifice made by Christ is not viewed as inadequate in any way and was sufficient for all time. In 'Abdu'l-Bahá's words, 'He [Christ] left nothing unfinished or incomplete' (*PUP* 367). The only inadequacy is that of humankind's response to Christ. If it were not for this inadequate response, Christ would not need to return and there would be no need to prophesy that He would. The appearance of Bahá'u'lláh and His suffering are further outpourings of God's grace despite our failures. 'Abdu'l-Bahá stated:

> If the followers of the Lord Christ had continued to follow out these principles with steadfast faithfulness, there would have been no need for a renewal of the Christian Message, no necessity for a reawakening of His people, for a great and glorious

civilization would now be ruling the world and the Kingdom of Heaven would have come on earth (PT 32).

Because of human nature, people eventually and inevitably turn away from the 'divinely illuminated precepts' (PT 32), the Faith of God, causing a 'winter' to fall 'upon the hearts of men' (PT 32). But 'Abdu'l-Bahá assures us:

> God leaves not His children comfortless, but, when the darkness of winter overshadows them, then again He sends His Messengers, the Prophets, with a renewal of the blessed spring. The Sun of Truth appears again on the horizon of the world shining into the eyes of those who sleep, awakening them to behold the glory of a new dawn (PT 32).

This is why God always sends Messengers or Prophets in every age, why Jesus prophesied His return, and why Bahá'u'lláh has come, and suffered, in fulfilment of those prophecies.

The Bahá'í view of Christ's return is thus a radical departure from the traditional views taught by the Christian clergy. Christ's return in visible 'power and great glory' concerns His power and glory made evident through the triumph of His Faith over His oppressors and human evils. Many priests and Christian ministers, however, do not expect Jesus to appear and suffer again. Such traditional views make it difficult for a Christian to investigate without bias the truth of Bahá'u'lláh. Therefore, it is necessary for Christians to free themselves from these presuppositions and to re-examine the Bible and Bahá'u'lláh's claims for themselves.

4 Fear God, O followers of the Spirit, and walk not in the footsteps of every divine that hath gone far astray.

COMMENTARY

Bahá'u'lláh counsels the Christians to fear God, and to exercise caution concerning divines. The phrase 'every divine' can have a wide meaning, including any ecclesiastics, clergy, priests, or theologians. This advice is perhaps intended to convey that one's spiritual fate, God's judgement, is not determined by the assurances given by the clergy. The context of the warning suggests that Christians should not accept blindly the views of the Church nor think it acceptable to reject Bahá'u'lláh's Cause simply because the religious leaders may have directed them to do so.

To 'fear God' means to have reverence for God's authority, to be mindful of the painful consequences of straying from God's will and of incurring God's judgement.[58] Bahá'u'lláh writes: 'Lay not aside the fear of God, O ye the learned of the world, and judge fairly the Cause of this unlettered One to Whom all the Books of God, the Protector, the Self-Subsisting have testified ... Will not the dread of Divine displeasure, the fear of Him Who hath no peer or equal arouse you?' (GWB 98).

One of Bahá'u'lláh's central teachings is that one should investigate truth independently and not see the

---

58. Bahá'u'lláh teaches that the 'essence of wisdom is the fear of God' (TB p. 155). This corresponds with biblical teaching (Ps. 111:10). 'The fear of God hath ever been a sure defence and a safe stronghold for all the peoples of the world. It is the chief cause of the protection of mankind, and the supreme instrument for its preservation' (ESW p. 27). This is probably because religious people do not believe evil actions escape God's omnipresence and judgement. Hence Bahá'u'lláh writes, 'Religion is, verily, the chief instrument for the establishment of order in the world, and of tranquillity amongst its peoples. The weakening of the pillars of religion hath strengthened the foolish and emboldened them, and made them more arrogant. Verily I say: The greater the decline of religion, the more grievous the waywardness of the ungodly' (ESW p. 28).

world merely through the eyes of others. Bahá'u'lláh warns that this is especially important in matters of faith and is essential for the establishment of justice. As we have seen with the example of the Pharisees, there is great danger in accepting the judgement of religious leaders without searching out the truth for oneself.

Although many religious leaders are genuinely pious and sincere, nevertheless Paul himself warned, 'For I know this, that after my departure savage wolves will come in among you, not sparing the flock' (Acts 20:29). Bahá'u'lláh states that the tribulation foretold in the Gospel (Matt. 24) signifies this day, a time when the Church is divided, when there is pervasive disagreement over the meaning of the Scriptures, and many self-seeking individuals have gained leadership of the Church. Bahá'u'lláh asks what tribulation 'is more grievous than that a soul seeking the truth, and wishing to attain unto the knowledge of God, should know not where to go for it and from whom to seek it?' (*KI* 31).

The Christian who turns to the leaders of the Church or the books of Christian scholars for guidance about the meaning of Scripture is confronted by a wide range of differing opinions. How can a Christian feel secure in judging Bahá'u'lláh by opinions and interpretations of the Bible about which Christians themselves disagree? Nowhere is there greater disagreement among Christians than over what the Bible teaches about the second coming of Christ.[59]

The person who put aside the opinions and objections of the Pharisees was able to judge the truth of Christ based

---

59. Even some conservative Christians who might otherwise uphold many of the same doctrinal views nevertheless often disagree about Christ's reappearance. Christians find themselves confronted, for example, by such theories as the partial rapture view, the post-tribulational rapture view, the mid-tribulational rapture view, the pre-tribulational rapture view, and so on (Floyd H. Barackman, *Practical Christian Theology*, pp. 337–9). See Carl F. H. Henry, ed., *Basic Christian Doctrines*, for theories concerning the millennium. Christian literature interpreting prophecies is vast. It would be short-sighted to accept the opinions of one interpreter and a formidable task to consider them all thoroughly.

on the evidences of Christ's own spirituality. Similarly, present-day disputes over the meaning of the Bible are often extraneous when we consider the evidence of Bahá'u'lláh.

5 Do ye imagine that He seeketh His own interests, when He hath, at all times, been threatened by the swords of the enemies; or that He seeketh the vanities of the world, after He hath been imprisoned in the most desolate of cities?
6 Be fair in your judgement and follow not the footsteps of the unjust.

COMMENTARY

The sincerity of Bahá'u'lláh's intentions is supported by His renunciation of wealth, comfort and security and His long suffering during years of persecution. Christ stated, 'And he who does not take his cross and follow after Me is not worthy of Me. He who finds his life will lose it, and he who loses his life for My sake will find it' (Matt. 10:38–9). Detachment in the path of God is a clear sign of devotion and sincerity.[60]

By continuing His claims, Bahá'u'lláh allowed Himself to be imprisoned in what He refers to as the 'most desolate of cities'. This place was 'Akká, today a small city in Israel. When Bahá'u'lláh was banished to 'Akká in 1868 it was a prison city, a remote Turkish penal colony, 'to which murderers, highway robbers and political agitators were consigned from all parts of the Turkish empire' (GPB 185). It was characterized by endemic

---

60. In the holy Book of Muḥammad, the Qur'án, it is written: 'Seek ye for death [martyrdom], if ye are sincere' (Qur'án 2:94). Bahá'u'lláh interprets this verse in the Kitáb-i-Íqán, see pp. 227–8.

diseases and the lack of any source of fresh water within its gates.[61] The conditions were so foul that some of Bahá'u'lláh's followers, who were exiled with Him, died within a short time.[62]

By pointing to His suffering, Bahá'u'lláh no doubt wants to compel Christians to consider His motives and His convictions. To enable Christians to judge Him, He does not engage in intellectual discussion over the interpretation of the Scriptures but, rather, appeals to the heart. Whatever we may think or whatever views we may accept, we all know in our own hearts that it is no ordinary belief or small amount of conviction that leads a person to sacrifice freely the benefits of this world and risk his or her life.

---

61. As time passed and people became acquainted with Bahá'u'lláh, their attitude towards Him changed. This change allowed for a small improvement to the city's water situation. The governor Aḥmad Big Tawfíq, largely through his association with 'Abdu'l-Bahá and having gained a favourable impression from Bahá'í literature, developed an admiration for Bahá'u'lláh. 'It was on the occasion of a long-sought audience with Bahá'u'lláh that, in response to a request for permission to render Him some service, the suggestion was made to him [Aḥmad Big Tawfíq] to restore the aqueduct which for thirty years had been allowed to fall into disuse – a suggestion which he immediately arose to carry out' (David S. Ruhe, *Door of Hope*, p. 52).

62. 'All fell sick, except two, shortly after their arrival. Malaria, dysentry, combined with the sultry heat, added to their miseries. Three succumbed, among them two brothers, who died the same night, "locked", as testified by Bahá'u'lláh, "in each other's arms"' (Shoghi Effendi, *GPB*, p. 187).

VII

1. Open the doors of your hearts.
2. He Who is the Spirit verily standeth before them.
3. Wherefore keep ye afar from Him who hath purposed to draw you nigh unto a Resplendent Spot?
4. Say:[63] We, in truth, have opened unto you the gates of the Kingdom.

COMMENTARY

In this passage Bahá'u'lláh asks Christians to open their hearts to Him. The emphasis now shifts further towards a clear proclamation of His claims. He states that He is, in fact, the same Spirit as Christ, and that through accepting Him they can experience for themselves the Kingdom of God.

The terminology Bahá'u'lláh uses is similar to the prophetic words found in the Apostle James's counsel:

> Therefore be patient, brethren, until the coming of the Lord. See how the farmer waits for the precious fruit of the earth, waiting patiently for it until it receives the early and latter rain. You also be patient.

---

63. Hans Küng writes that the Qur'án's use of the word 'Say' corresponds to the Old Testament's 'Thus says the Lord' (*Christianity and the World Religions*, p. 26). It suggests a divine command to accept or acknowledge that this is from God.

Establish your hearts, for the coming of the Lord is at hand. Do not grumble against one another, brethren, lest you be condemned. Behold, the Judge is standing at the Door! (Jas: 5:7–9).

With the words, 'He Who is the Spirit' standing before the 'doors of your heart' He asserts His unity with the Spirit of Christ (KI 152–3). Bahá'u'lláh's words indicate that His claim is Messianic and that He is summoning Christians to accept Him.

The phrase, 'Open the doors of your hearts', implies that perception of the truth is not by intellect alone but must be accompanied by pure motives, suggesting a reliance on spiritual perception. The emphasis on heartfelt discernment was expressed by Christ when He taught that 'Blessed are the pure in heart, for they shall see God' (Matt. 5:8). This prerequisite for spiritual discernment was also expressed in the Hebrew Scriptures, 'Who may ascend into the hill of the LORD? ... He who has clean hands and a pure heart, who has not lifted up his soul to an idol, nor sworn deceitfully. He shall receive blessings from the LORD, and righteousness from the God of his salvation.' (Ps. 24:3–5)

The person who is concerned about what others may think, or about personal losses that may result, has not purified his or her heart. Purity of heart is freedom from all such concerns when seeking the truth. Because this is so essential to spiritual life, Bahá'u'lláh teaches, 'My first counsel is this: Possess a pure, kindly and radiant heart, that thine may be a sovereignty ancient, imperishable and everlasting' (HWA 3).[64]

64. It may be unwise for a commentator to tackle this controversy, but it is the understanding of this writer that references to purity of heart and spiritual perception need not imply any extra-sensory perception or some unfamiliar faculty of the soul. It seems more probable that such Scriptures simply mean that one should be characterized by spiritual virtues in order to best arrive at the truth. Honesty, impartiality and patience are among the many obvious requirements for justice in a court of law. Similarly, the quest for religious truth certainly demands no less. In the Kitáb-i-Íqán, Bahá'u'lláh emphasizes virtues and especially freedom from any prejudice when seeking the truth (KI pp. 192–200).

The saying that the 'gates of the Kingdom' have been opened may mean the spiritual Kingdom of God which Christ spoke of and ushered in (Matt. 12:28) as well as that which Christ prayed for, 'Your kingdom come. Your will be done on earth as it is in heaven' (Luke 11:2). This will be discussed further in the commentary to paragraph XXIV.

5 Will ye bar the doors of your house in My face?[65]
6 This indeed is naught but a grievous error.
7 He, verily, hath again come down from heaven, even as He came down from it the first time.
8 Beware lest ye dispute that which He proclaimeth, even as the people before you disputed His utterances.
9 Thus instructeth you the True One,[66] could ye but perceive it.

COMMENTARY

Bahá'u'lláh's claim that He 'hath again come down from heaven' is intended to convey that His Revelation is from God. This is an especially significant claim because of its parallel to the claim of Christ recorded in the Gospel. Christ stated, 'For I come down from heaven, not to do My own will, but the will of Him that sent Me' (John 6:38). Because many Christians believe Christ will literally return in the clouds, descending from the physical heavens, it is natural that Christians object to Bahá'u'lláh's claims. Christ's own words indicate that to come down from heaven represents a spiritual occurrence, since He was Himself born on earth. Therefore, Bahá'u'lláh warns Christians not to dispute with Him

---

65. Cf. Matt. 24:42–4.
66. The 'True One' refers to Bahá'u'lláh (Shoghi Effendi, PDC, p. 35).

even as the Gospel records the Jews disputed with Christ. 'The Jews then murmured against Him, because He said, "I am the bread which came down from heaven." And they said, "Is not this Jesus son of Joseph, whose father and mother we know? How is it that He says, 'I have come down from heaven'?"' (John 6:41–2). The Pharisees neither perceived the divinity of Christ nor understood the symbolism Christ used to express that divine reality.

'Abdu'l-Bahá explains Christ's words in this way:

> Notice ... that it is said that Christ came from heaven, though He came from the womb of Mary, and His body was born of Mary. It is clear, then, that when it is said that the Son of man is come from heaven, this has not an outward but an inward signification; it is a spiritual, not a material, fact. The meaning is that though, apparently, Christ was born from the womb of Mary, in reality He came from heaven, from the centre of the Sun of Reality, from the Divine World, and the Spiritual Kingdom. And as it has become evident that Christ came from the spiritual heaven of the Divine Kingdom, therefore His disappearance under the earth for three days has an inner signification, and is not an outward fact. In the same way, His resurrection from the interior of the earth is also symbolic; it is a spiritual and divine fact, and not material; and likewise His ascension to heaven is a spiritual and not material ascension.
>
> Besides these explanations, it has been established and proved by science that the visible heaven is a limitless area, void and empty, where innumerable stars and planets revolve (*SAQ* ch. 23).

'Abdu'l-Bahá's interpretation of Christ's resurrection and return is a radical departure from the traditional literal interpretations of many Christians. However, it should be emphasized that 'Abdu'l-Bahá does not deny or wish to devalue the resurrection or return of Christ; He insists that these are facts but that they are 'spiritual and divine' in nature, and not material occurrences that take place in the sky.

The resurrection and return of Christ are both important realities from the Bahá'í point of view. For example, Paul states that, 'if Christ is not risen, then our preaching is vain and your faith is also vain' (1 Cor. 15:14). Many Christians interpret this to mean a physical resurrection. The Bahá'í view affirms the importance of the resurrection, but without assuming a literal interpretation. A person is spiritually dead unless raised to life by the Word of God. When a person is raised from the death of disbelief to the life of faith, he or she is resurrected (*PUP* 182). Without this resurrection to the spiritual life, as Paul says, one's 'faith is vain'.

The resurrection of Christ symbolizes how the faith of Christ lives on. The death of Christ represents the spiritual death of 'the body of Christ', which the Scriptures explain to be the believers (1 Cor. 12:27). This death of the Church occurred because of the doubts and disbelief of the Apostles who fled after Christ was crucified. However, the stumbling block of His physical death (1 Cor. 1:22–4) was rolled back from the tomb of disbelief when the Faith of Christ was resurrected in the hearts of the Apostles. Thus, from a Bahá'í point of view, the resurrection of Christ was the establishment of His Church (*SAQ* ch. 23).[67]

This is a belief that many Christians find impossible to accept, but as Bahá'u'lláh points out, the Pharisees also found it impossible to accept that Christ had come down from heaven. Christians point to the Gospel narratives to argue that the resurrection was literal even as the Pharisees pointed to Jesus's birth on earth and rejected His teaching that He came from heaven.

Bahá'u'lláh's claim that, 'He, verily, hath again come down from heaven, even as He came down from it the

---

67. For additional explanations of the biblical resurrection narratives based on Bahá'í exegesis, see Michael W. Sours, *Preparing for a Bahá'í-Christian Dialogue*, vol. 2, chs. 11–12 (forthcoming).

first time', is a proclamation of His divinity, but it is also an exhortation to Christians to see the spiritual significance of the Scriptures and recognize that He is the fulfilment of Christ's prophecies.

VIII

1 The river Jordan is joined to the Most Great Ocean, and the Son, in the holy vale, crieth out: 'Here am I, here am I, O Lord, my God!', whilst Sinai circleth round the House, and the Burning Bush calleth aloud: 'He Who is the Desired One is come in His transcendent majesty.'

COMMENTARY

It seems likely, here, that Bahá'u'lláh is expressing the oneness of the Revelation of Jesus with His own Revelation, or, in fact, proclaiming that the Gospel itself testifies to this unity between His Cause and that of Christ. The Revelation of Jesus is symbolized by the River Jordan, which is joined with His Revelation, symbolized as the Most Great Ocean. The phrase, 'Most Great Ocean' expresses the greatness and fullness of Bahá'u'lláh's Revelation and appears many times in His writings.[68] The phrase also suggests the fulfilment of the prophecy, 'For the earth shall be full of the knowledge of the Lord, as the waters cover the sea' (Isa. 11:9).

The River Jordan is where John the Baptist baptized his

---

68. E.g. *GWB*, pp. 33, 59, 71 and 104.

followers and, eventually, Jesus (Mark 1:5–10).[69] In the Bible water is often associated with the knowledge or Revelation of God. For example, Christ said, 'He Who believes in Me, as the Scripture has said, out of his heart will flow rivers of living water' (John 7:38, and see also 4:10).

This type of poetic and mystical language defies precise analysis. We can only guess at some of the possible meanings. It may be that 'the Son, in the holy vale', crying out: 'Here am I,[70] here am I, O Lord, My God!', is meant to indicate how the Revelation of Christ, that is the Gospel or the Spirit of Christ, mystically calls out in acknowledgement of Bahá'u'lláh's truth. Or more simply, it may be a way of saying that the words of Christ prophesy and serve to affirm Bahá'u'lláh's advent (e.g. Matt. 24; John 16). The words, 'Here am I', are found frequently in the Old Testament (e.g. Gen. 22:1, 7, 11; Exod. 3:4).[71]

The 'Son' most probably means Jesus and 'the holy vale' may signify the divinely appointed place of God's Revelation.[72] 'Sinai' may be intended here to mean the habitation of the Lord (Exod. 24:16; see Lawḥ-i-Aqdas

69. 'No other river has more biblical allusions and significance' (*New Bible Dictionary*, p. 615). 'The parallelism between the Joshua who led the Old Israel across the Jordan into the Promised Land and the Lord Jesus who brings his New Israel through the waters of baptism into their heavenly inheritance did not escape the Fathers of the early Church' (Alan Richardson, ed., *A Theological Word Book of the Bible*, p. 116).

70. In the Book of Revelation, Jesus calls out to the Church in Laodicea with these words, 'Here I am! I stand at the door and knock. If anyone hears my voice and opens the door, I will go in and eat with him, and he with me' (Rev. 3:19, NIV).

71. In a letter to this writer the Bahá'í scholar Stephen Lambden conveyed that the original Arabic expression in the *Lawḥ-i-Aqdas* 'is an imperative expression of the desire to serve and to obey'. This understanding is reflected in the earlier translation of the *Lawḥ-i-Aqdas*, in which the phrase, 'Here am I', is rendered, 'I am ready'. This understanding of the Arabic is equally applicable to the Hebrew expression found in the Bible.

72. Stephen Lambden has pointed out that 'the expression "holy vale" is rooted in the Qur'ánic account of the [Sinaitic] call of Moses.' Lambden writes, 'A wide range of spiritual senses is accorded the expression "the holy vale" in Bábí and Bahá'í Scripture. Just as Moses stood in the "holy vale" when He was commissioned by God at the time of the "burning bush"/Sinai experience or vision, it seems that Jesus is pictured [in the *Lawḥ-i-Aqdas*] as standing in the "holy vale" (the new Sinai now symbolized by 'Akká, the place of Bahá'u'lláh's imprisonment and exile) crying out in recognition of the Manifestation of God

XI:3), the law or source of the law of God, and the Revelation of Moses. Paul speaks of Sinai as an allegory for the covenant of Moses (Gal. 4:24). The reference to Sinai circling the House[73] may be an allusion to the prophecies of Isaiah, 'Now it will come to pass in the latter days that the mountain of the Lord's House shall be established on the top of the mountains, and shall be exalted above the hills; and all nations shall flow unto it' (Isa. 2:2). Thus, the Son and the Burning Bush proclaiming and acknowledging Bahá'u'lláh's advent suggest that, by turning to the Scriptures of the Bible, one will find confirmation of Bahá'u'lláh's claims. These words, expressing as they do the unity of His Revelation with the Scriptures of the past, represent the first of many allusions to the prophesies of the Bible which follow in this paragraph.

2 Say, Lo! The Father is come, and that which ye were promised in the Kingdom is fulfilled!

COMMENTARY

In this verse Bahá'u'lláh identifies Himself as the 'Father'. Bahá'ís view this as symbolic of God, making no assertion

---

as Bahá'u'lláh.' Lambden has observed that the Arabic expression 'holy vale' (al-wád al-muqaddas) in the Lawḥ-i-Aqdas is derived from the Qur'án (see Qur'án 20:12 and 79:16). Most translators (e.g. Rodwell, Arberry) render the Arabic in English as 'holy valley', as it appears in the earlier translation of the Lawḥ-i-Aqdas, or 'sacred valley' (e.g. Sale, Shakir, Yusuf Ali). The Qur'án reads 'sacred valley Tuwa' (Qur'án 20:12) and 'sacred valley of Tuwa' (Qur'án 79:16; see also ESW, pp. 117–18). The Muslim commentator Yusuf Ali expresses the view that the word 'Tuwa', also transliterated 'Towa', and 'Towah', is the name of the valley just below Mount Sinai (See A. Yusuf Ali, trans., The Holy Qur'án, note 2544). In the Kitáb-i-Íqán, Bahá'u'lláh writes: 'Moses entered the holy vale, situated in the wilderness of Sinai, and there beheld the vision of the King of glory from the "Tree that belongeth neither to the East nor to the West"' (p. 54). Bahá'u'lláh's overall account given in the Kitáb-i-Íqán suggests a mystic or spiritual portrait of the event rather than a purely historical-geographical description. It is likely that this is the intention in the Lawḥ-i-Aqdas as well.

73. In another instance Bahá'u'lláh writes, 'Sinai is circling around the Day Spring of Revelation' (GWB p. 211).

that Bahá'u'lláh is God in essence, but rather a Manifestation of the attributes of God. The name 'Father' emphasizes those attributes of God manifest in Bahá'u'lláh that could be characterized as fatherly in nature. 'That which ye were promised in the Kingdom is fulfilled' may mean the prophecies of the Bible, promised when the Gospel was originally preached.

One of the names Isaiah attributes to the Messiah is 'Everlasting Father' (Isa. 9:6). Also, Christ stated that the 'Son of man' will come in the 'glory of His Father' (Mark 8:38). Some Bahá'ís express the view that this name signifies Bahá'u'lláh's station as One who brings together the family of all humankind, much as a shepherd gathers together his sheep. This is especially demonstrated in Bahá'u'lláh's teachings that all humankind is one, that the world's great religions come from the same God, and that people must give up their prejudices and work together. Christ stated, 'And other sheep I have which are not of this fold; them also I must bring, and they will hear My voice; and there will be one flock and one shepherd' (John 10:16). One understanding of this verse is that 'the other sheep' refers to people of other religions who are not Christians and who are now being brought together in the Bahá'í Faith.[74]

Another explanation, that of Mírzá Abu'l-Faḍl, is recounted by Adib Taherzadeh in his book *The Revelation of Bahá'u'lláh*. In a dialogue that took place in 1887, with the Reverend Dr Robert Bruce, Abu'l-Faḍl explains:

> These words [Isa. 9:6] testified that a son would be born who would save the Children of Israel from abasement and misery, and would be described by the following attributes: first, a 'Counsellor' who

---

74. This view was popularized among Bahá'ís by William Sears in his book *The Wine of Astonishment*, pp. 82–96.

counsels the people; second, 'the mighty God' which means the Supreme Manifestation of God and the greatest Primal Word;[75] third, 'the everlasting Father', through whom all human beings from the beginning till the end have been created and born of His sovereignty and omnipotence;[76] fourth, 'the Prince of Peace', through whose Revelation the foundation of the oneness and unity of the human race would be laid, and the ills of discord and war which cause the destruction of the world and the degradation of the human race would be eliminated.

From this clear and explicit verse it is clear that the 'Heavenly Father' will appear in the form of the human temple, will be born of a mother and be known by the Greatest Name. It appears that in other passages of the Holy Books one may not be able to find a statement about the 'Heavenly Father' as explicit and evident as this one.[77]

Christians generally accept that this verse, in Isaiah, refers to Christ. While it is true that this verse can be interpreted as applicable to either the first or second advent of Christ, the words of the following verse 'of the increase of his government and peace there will be no end' (Isa. 9:7), if interpreted outwardly, seem to refer especially to the second advent, which is a view that many Christians also acknowledge.[78]

---

75. 'Primal word' means that the Manifestation is the Word of God. This suggests both the pre-existence of the Manifestations as well as the creative nature of God's Word as expressed in John 1:1,14.
76. This concerns spiritual creation and birth. In 1 Pet. 1:23, it is written that we are born again 'through the word of God'. See also John 1:12–13.
77. Adib Taherzadeh, The Revelation of Bahá'u'lláh, vol. IV, p. 268.
78. Alfred and John Martin, Isaiah: The Glory of the Messiah, p. 107.

3 This is the Word which the Son concealed, when to those around Him He said: 'Ye cannot bear it now.'
4 And when the appointed time was fulfilled and the Hour had struck, the Word shone forth above the horizon of the Will of God.

COMMENTARY

Bahá'u'lláh indicates here that Jesus's words, 'I still have many things to say to you, but you cannot bear them now' (John 16:12), are in fact a prophecy about His Revelation. This assertion indicates that Bahá'u'lláh's message would have been more than people could have understood or accepted in the time of Christ. Moreover, He asserts, that message is now given to the world and the 'appointed time' has come.

This prophecy suggests that one must exercise humility in judging Bahá'u'lláh's Revelation. Christianity today still reflects and, in many cases, adheres to beliefs drawn up in creeds and doctrines dating back to the first centuries following Christ. Christ had many things to say, but the people could not bear them at that time. Therefore, it is not surprising that, even today, Christians who adhere to the traditional views of the Church find it hard to accept Bahá'u'lláh's teachings.

It is not difficult to see that many of Bahá'u'lláh's teachings would have been impracticable or misunderstood two thousand years ago. Given the relative geographical isolation, general illiteracy and the lack of effective transport or communications technology which characterized past societies, how could the type of world unity alluded to in the prophecies of Scripture be established? How would such a world receive Bahá'u'lláh's teachings concerning the validity and tolerance of other religions, the equality of men and women, the unity of science and religion, and the establishment of a universal language and a world tribunal? Furthermore, Bahá'u'lláh abrogates such institutions as slavery, the priesthood, elaborate religious ceremonies, and what are now outmoded laws of former ages. This is to say nothing of the broad theological content of Bahá'u'lláh's writings which would no doubt have been revolutionary for past ages.

In the phrase, 'the Word shone forth above the horizon of the will of God', the use of the word 'horizon' is rooted in the ancient metaphor of light, signifying truth. The words of Jesus suggest this metaphor, 'As long as I am in the world, I am the light of the world' (John 9:5). The sun is often used to represent God or the Prophets as the greatest light guiding humankind. The horizon signifies the point where this light first appears in the world. Use of this metaphor is eloquently expressed in these words of 'Abdu'l-Bahá which we referred to earlier:

> God leaves not His Children comfortless, but, when the darkness of winter overshadows them, then again He sends His Messengers, the Prophets, with a renewal of the blessed spring. The Sun of Truth appears again on the horizon of the world shining into the eyes of those who sleep, awaking them to behold the glory of a new dawn. Then again will the tree of humanity blossom and bring forth the fruit of righteousness for the healing of the nations (PT 32).

In another talk 'Abdu'l-Bahá stated: 'Christ was the Sun of Reality which shone from the heavenly horizon of Christianity, training, protecting, confirming minds, souls and spirits until they came into harmony with the divine Kingdom.' (PUP 271).

'Horizon' in the particular context of 'the will of God' emphasizes the divinely ordained nature of Bahá'u'lláh's appearance in the world. That is to say His appearance is by God's will and not of human will.

5 Beware, O followers of the Son, that ye cast it not behind your backs.
6 Take ye fast hold of it.
7 Better is this for you than all that ye possess.
8 Verily He is nigh unto them that do good.

COMMENTARY

The context of these verses suggests the greatness of what Christ promised and the importance of heeding the prophecies of the Bible. Bahá'u'lláh calls Christians to accept Him and to remain steadfast in His Cause. This, He says, will be better for them than holding on to what they possess. The words 'all that ye possess' may have a very wide meaning encompassing worldly possessions, ideological concerns, and the institutions of the Church. For the Christian priests in particular, 'all that ye possess' may also include their congregations. The message reflects the truth Jesus expressed with these words, 'For what will it profit a man if he gains the whole world, and loses his own soul?' (Mark 8:36; see also John 6:63).

Bahá'u'lláh says, 'He is nigh unto them that do good'. Christ told His followers: 'If you abide in My word, you are My disciples indeed. And you shall know the truth' (John 8:31–2). These words suggest that the sincere follower whose aim is to follow the truth will not be hindered from recognizing Bahá'u'lláh by corrupt pursuits, worldly leadership, and material wealth. One way to know the divinity of Bahá'u'lláh's teachings, and perhaps the most certain way, is to experience that divinity for oneself by practising the teachings. Christ expressed this method to the people of His time in this passage: 'If anyone wants to do His will, he shall know concerning the teachings, whether it is from God or whether I speak on My own authority' (John 7:17, RV). Throughout the Gospel we are told that our actions and, even more, our intentions, affect our ability to see the truth and influence our closeness to God. John wrote,

'Now he who keeps His commandments abides in Him, and He in him' (1 John 3:24; see also 1 John 3:6; Jas. 2:26).

9 The hour which We had concealed from the knowledge of the peoples of the earth and of the favoured angels[79] hath come to pass.

COMMENTARY

Here Bahá'u'lláh indicates the fulfilment of the time Christ foretold with these words: 'But of that day and hour no one knows, neither the angels in heaven, nor the Son, but only the Father' (Mark 13:32). Bahá'u'lláh may have chosen to refer to this prophecy because it challenges certain objections to His claims. Christian commentators have often devised elaborate scenarios based on the interpretation of prophecies. In these interpretations they establish things that must occur before the coming of Christ. Thus, a Christian may raise the objection to Bahá'u'lláh that certain signs must first appear in a certain way before he or she will investigate His claims.[80] Christ's statement that 'of that day and hour no one knows' indicates that the faithful believer should remain open-minded and humble when attempting to interpret prophecy and establish when Christ will appear. It is

---

79. In the *Kitáb-i-Íqán*, Bahá'u'lláh explains that by 'angels' is meant individuals who 'reinforced by the power of the spirit, have consumed, with the fire of the love of God, all human traits and limitations, and have clothed themselves with the attributes of the most exalted Beings' (*KI* pp. 78–9). 'Abdu'l-Bahá stated to a small group of Bahá'ís in 1912: 'Array yourselves in the perfection of divine virtues. I hope you may be quickened and vivified by the breaths of the Holy Spirit. Then shall ye indeed become the angels of the heaven whom Christ promised would appear in this Day [Matt. 24:31, 25:31] to gather the harvest of divine planting. This is my hope. This is my prayer for you' (*PUP* p. 7).

80. Some Christians have prerequisites such as that the Dome of the Rock (Kubbet es-Sakhra) in Jerusalem must be destroyed and the Jewish Temple rebuilt, or the Soviet Army must invade Israel. Views of this type can be found in such books as Hal Lindsey's *The Late Great Planet Earth*. See footnote 142 (p. 163).

possible to interpret prophecy correctly. However, if Christ has returned at an unexpected time, it should be understood that the interpretation was wrong rather than taking it as an indication that He should be rejected.

10 Say, verily, He hath testified of Me, and I do testify of Him.

COMMENTARY

Bahá'u'lláh asserts that the words of Jesus, recorded in the Gospel, testify to His Cause and that He also testifies to the truth of Christ.

Christ prophesied that, 'He will glorify Me, for He will take of what is mine and declare it to you. All things that the Father has are Mine. Therefore I said that He will take of Mine and declare it to you' (John 16:14–15). There are many passages in Bahá'u'lláh's writings where He testifies to the truth and reality of Christ as well as to the Gospel of Christ. In one example Bahá'u'lláh writes that the sacrifice of Christ changed the world: 'Know thou that when the Son of Man yielded up His breath to God, the whole creation wept with a great weeping. By sacrificing Himself, however, a fresh capacity was infused into all created things' (GWB 85). In another case Bahá'u'lláh writes a detailed defence of the genuineness of the Gospel in which He says: 'Reflect: the words of the verses themselves eloquently testify to the truth that they are of God' (KI 84; see also 86–9).[81] In another reference, the

---

81. This does not mean, of course, that the Gospel is of God merely because the Gospel says it is of God. Such an argument would be fallacious reasoning. Rather the meaning is that the message and attributes of God are revealed in the message of the Gospel, thus indicating that it is of God.

Bahá'í writings state that 'the divine inspiration of the Gospel is fully recognized' (PDC 109).[82]

11 Indeed, He hath purposed no one other than Me.
12 Unto this beareth witness every fair-minded and understanding soul.

COMMENTARY

The prophecies Bahá'u'lláh has alluded to, which can be found in John 14:26, 15:26 and 16:7–15, are traditionally believed by many Christians to be references to the Holy Spirit that descended on the Apostles as recorded in Acts 2. With the words, 'He hath purposed no one other than Me', Bahá'u'lláh is pointing out that Jesus's words in John 16, alluded to above, are, in fact, prophecies concerning Him. Bahá'u'lláh expresses the conviction that, if appraised in a 'fair-minded' way, it will be acknowledged that Christ is referring to Him. This could also be applied more generally to the overall prophetic statements of Jesus recorded in the Gospel.

The Bahá'í view does not dispute that the Holy Spirit descended on the Apostles as recorded in Acts 2. However, 'Abdu'l-Bahá explains, 'consider carefully that from these words, "for he shall not speak of himself; but whatsoever he shall hear, that shall he speak"; it is clear that the Spirit of Truth is embodied in a man who has individuality, who has ears to hear and a tongue to speak' (SAQ 125; see also PUP 41–2).

Although Bahá'ís do accept that many other prophecies refer to Bahá'u'lláh, including passages in the Book of

---

82. In the Kitáb-i-Íqán, Bahá'u'lláh writes a forceful defence of the Bible, particularly the Gospel. Bahá'u'lláh rejects the radical Islamic polemics against the genuineness of the Gospel, which He attributes to their misunderstandings of both the Qur'án and the Gospel, pp. 83–90.

Revelation, Bahá'u'lláh has chosen to emphasize verses which almost any seeker can grasp.[83] These prophecies (John 14:15–16, 16:12), provide the Christian with authoritative words from Christ for considering the truth of Bahá'u'lláh. It is perhaps significant that these words point to the need for humility rather than a reliance on a scholarly knowledge of all the complex prophecies of the Bible. We also find that Bahá'u'lláh fulfils the prophecy that He will testify to the truth of Christ. The Scriptures testify to Him and He testifies to the Scriptures. This makes it clear that Bahá'u'lláh sees Himself in the successive unfolding of God's plan that is revealed in the Bible.

---

83. The Christian commentator L. L. Morris writes that the Book of Revelation 'abounds in symbolism of a type that we do not use and to which we no longer possess the key' (*New Bible Dictionary*, p. 1027).

IX

1 Though beset with countless afflictions, We summon the people unto God, the Lord of names.

COMMENTARY

Despite a long ministry spent in exile (GPB 106–7), being imprisoned repeatedly (GPB 71, 179), and being poisoned by His adversaries (GPB 72, 165–6), Bahá'u'lláh persevered in proclaiming His Cause. This singular steadfastness to the service of God is a sign supporting His claims.

One of the principal characteristics of a Prophet is that He summons the people back to God. If we examine the life and teachings of Bahá'u'lláh we find that, like Christ and the Prophets of Israel, Bahá'u'lláh continually counsels people to devote themselves to God and to accept the authority of God:

> Let him who will, acknowledge the truth of My words; and as to him that willeth not, let him turn aside. My sole duty is to remind you of your failure in duty towards the Cause of God, if perchance ye may be of them that heed My warning. Wherefore, hearken ye unto My speech, and return ye to God and repent, that He, through His grace, may have mercy upon you, may wash away your sins, and forgive your trespasses. The greatness of His mercy

surpasseth the fury of His wrath, and His grace encompasseth all who have been called into being and clothed with the robe of life, be they of the past or of the future (*GWB* 130).

The reference to God as the 'Lord of names' signifies that God possesses all divine attributes in the most absolute and greatest degree.[84] 'Abdu'l-Bahá explains:

The reality of Divinity is characterized by certain names and attributes. Among these names are Creator, Resuscitator, Provider, the All-Present, Almighty, Omniscient and Giver. These names and attributes of Divinity are eternal and not accidental. This is a very subtle point which demands close attention. Their existence is proved and necessitated by the appearance of phenomena. For example, Creator presupposes creation, Resuscitator implies resuscitation, Provider necessitates provision; otherwise, these would be empty and impossible names. Merciful evidences an object upon which mercy is bestowed. If mercy were not manifest, this attribute of God would not be realized (*PUP* 271-2).

---

84. This type of terminology is used in the Qur'án in such verses as: 'The most beautiful names belong to God' (7:180); 'He is God, the Creator, the Evolver, the Bestower of Forms. To Him belong the Most Beautiful of Names: Whatever is in the heavens and on earth, doth declare His praises and glory: and He is the Exalted in Might, the Wise' (59:24). What is generally referred to as the names of God in Islamic and Bahá'í writing, Christians would speak of as attributes of God. This is the same meaning Bahá'ís intend with the word 'names'. A Christian outline of the attributes of God can be found in Barackman's *Practical Christian Theology*, pp. 31-8. See also the names of God, *New Bible Dictionary*, pp. 429-30, 812-13.

2 Say, strive ye to attain that which ye have been promised in the Books of God, and walk not in the way of the ignorant.

COMMENTARY

With the words 'strive ye' Bahá'u'lláh challenges the belief that the second coming of Christ and the Kingdom of God foretold in the Scriptures will simply appear around us as a matter of observation. Rather, as is indicated in Bahá'u'lláh's writings, humankind must strive to recognize the truth and follow His teachings. Bahá'u'lláh teaches that people must take responsibility to spiritualize their lives individually, as well as collectively, in the world. He outlines a path in His teachings, a divinely prescribed and necessary remedy for the world's problems; humankind, however, must respond in order to benefit from it (*GWB* 213). Christ states, 'Strive to enter through the narrow gate, for many, I say to you, will seek to enter and will not be able' (Luke 13:24), and in another passage, 'The kingdom of God does not come with observation; nor will they say, "See here!" or "See there!" For indeed, the kingdom of God is within you' (Luke 17:20–1).

The promises recorded in the Bible, which Bahá'u'lláh refers to, are far too numerous to examine in this commentary. However, it should be noted that Bahá'u'lláh generally speaks of fulfilment in a way that reflects a spiritual understanding and not a strictly literal, material interpretation. For example, it is prophesied that, 'The wolf and the lamb shall feed together' (Isa. 65:25). Some Christians expect that this will literally occur when Christ returns, whereas 'Abdu'l-Bahá explains:

> It means that fierce and contending religions, hostile creeds and divergent beliefs will reconcile and associate, notwithstanding their former hatreds and antagonism. Through the liberalism of human atti-

tude demanded in this radiant century they will blend together in perfect fellowship and love. This is the spirit and meaning of Isaiah's words. There will never be a day when this prophecy will come to pass literally, for these animals by their natures cannot mingle and associate in kindness and love. Therefore, this prophecy symbolizes the unity and agreement of races, nations and peoples who will come together in attitudes of intelligence, illumination and spirituality (*PUP* 369–70).[85]

'Abdu'l-Bahá goes on to say that this day has, in fact, dawned and is becoming more and more a reality. In one of His talks, 'Abdu'l-Bahá points out that this type of unity is already apparent among the followers of Bahá'u'lláh:

Antagonism and strife have passed away; love and agreement have taken the place of hatred and animosity. Furthermore, those souls who have followed Bahá'u'lláh and attained this condition of fellowship and affiliation are Muslims, Jews, Christians, Zoroastrians, Buddhists, Nestorians, Sunnites, Shi'ites and others. No discord exists among them. This is a proof of the possibility of the unification among the religionists of the world through practical means (*PUP* 234; see also 341).

Another example of how Bahá'ís understand the fulfilment of biblical prophecies can be seen with the prophecies recorded in the Book of Revelation: 'And God will wipe away every tear from their eyes; there shall be no more death, nor sorrow, nor crying; and there shall be no more pain, for the former things have passed away' (Rev. 21:4). Some Christians await a literal fulfilment of this

---

85. Interpreting Isaiah, the popular evangelist Billy Graham writes in his best-selling book, *Approaching Hoofbeats*, 'So transformed will the prevailing order be that even the animal world will be completely tamed' (p. 260).

passage.[86] However, 'Abdu'l-Bahá writes that it has been fulfilled with the advent of Bahá'u'lláh (*SWA* 12–13). This suggests that the prophecy has a spiritual significance that pertains to the life of faith (*KI* 114). Biblical support for this view can be found in the words of Paul, who indicates that such a condition has occurred in Paul's time with those who have accepted Christ: 'Therefore, if anyone is in Christ, he is a new creation; old things have passed away; behold, all things have become new' (2 Cor. 5:17). And, in another passage, Paul speaks of how they were 'dead in trespasses' before their conversion to Christianity, but God made them 'alive together with Christ' and 'raised us up together, and made us sit together in the heavenly places in Christ Jesus' (Eph. 2: 4–6).

The words 'walk not in the way of the ignorant' may be Bahá'u'lláh's challenge to those who would assert that such prophecies are to be understood literally.

3 My body hath endured imprisonment that ye may be released from the bondage of self.

COMMENTARY

Here Bahá'u'lláh contrasts the imprisonment He was made to suffer with the spiritual liberation that He has offered to humankind. This passage is particularly significant because Bahá'u'lláh is pointing out how He has suffered as a ransom for humankind, that is, He suffers so that we may not have to suffer. Bahá'u'lláh teaches that this is characteristic of all Manifestations of God (*GWB*

---

86. Billy Graham writes that when Christ returns, 'He will remove all deformities and handicaps. At that time there'll be no designated spots on parking lots, or graduated ramps on buildings, for the handicapped. There will be no blindness, deafness, muteness, paralysis – no need for eyeglasses, hearing aids, speech therapy, wheelchairs, crutches, or white canes' (Ibid., p. 261).

75–6). They all spread the word of God and are consequently persecuted by those whose actions and beliefs they challenge. They persevere so that the transcendence of God's word may become evident and their examples may awaken the conscience and spirit within the people of the world. In this way they are a ransom for the world and are the way by which the world is drawn back to God. Bahá'u'lláh states:

> It is Our wish and desire that every one of you may become a source of all goodness unto men, and an example of uprightness to mankind. Beware lest ye prefer yourselves above your neighbours. Fix your gaze upon Him Who is the Temple of God amongst men. He, in truth, hath offered up His life as a ransom for the redemption of the world. He verily, is the All-Bountiful, the Gracious, the Most High (*GWB* 315).

4 Set your faces then towards His countenance and follow not the footsteps of every hostile oppressor.

5 Verily, He hath consented to be sorely abased that ye may attain unto glory, and yet, ye are disporting yourselves in the vale of heedlessness.

6 He, in truth, liveth in the most desolate of abodes for your sakes, whilst ye dwell in your palaces.

COMMENTARY

Bahá'u'lláh is calling Christians to consider whether those who are leading the people are really following a spiritual path. This may be a warning to Christians, and to believers in general, not to become tools of those who oppress innocent people. This warning may concern the mistake of following religious leaders who, like the Pharisees at the time of Christ, turned the people against the Messiah they had awaited. The phrase 'hostile oppressors', suggests persons who seek only their own interests without regard for the suffering they cause other people, directly or indirectly. It may include political and religious leaders who, when not blatantly tyrannical, are nevertheless characterized by a pervasive indifference to the world's suffering, the evils of racial prejudice, extremes of poverty, and the loss of life in war after war. He exposes the real desires of those who have rejected Him by contrasting their affluent lifestyles with the condition He has had to accept, 'the most desolate of abodes', in order to promote the Word of God.

Bahá'u'lláh states that, 'He hath consented to be sorely abased' so that we 'may attain unto glory'. By this is meant that He has endured suffering so as to spread the teachings of God for the betterment of others. The abasement He refers to concerns the outward appearance of His life, resulting from His exiles and imprisonments; it does not refer to His spiritual condition which was never abased.

The teachings for which He has suffered are the real means by which people 'may attain to glory'. 'Abdu'l-Bahá explains:

> If man lives up to these divine commandments, this world of earth shall be transformed into the world of heaven, and this material sphere shall be converted into a paradise of glory. It is my hope that you may become successful on this high calling so that like brilliant lamps you may cast light upon the world of humanity and quicken and stir the body of existence like unto a spirit of life. This is eternal glory (PUP 470).

In another talk, He stated: 'Man must be lofty in endeavour. He must seek to become heavenly and spiritual, to find the pathway to the threshold of God and become acceptable in the sight of God. This is eternal glory – to be near to God' (*PUP* 186).

X

1 Say, did ye not hearken to the Voice of the Crier, calling aloud in the wilderness of the Bayán, bearing unto you the glad tidings of the coming of your Lord, the All-Merciful?

COMMENTARY

This passage refers to the Báb (1819–50) who heralded the Cause of Bahá'u'lláh.[87] Although the Báb is regarded by Bahá'ís as an independent Prophet of God, meaning the Founder of His own Faith (i.e. the Bábí Faith), He is viewed in relation to Bahá'u'lláh as a herald, similar to John the Baptist, who heralded Christ's appearance. Bahá'u'lláh characterizes the Báb in the language used by Isaiah, 'The voice of one crying in the wilderness: "Prepare

---

87. The scholar E. G. Browne writes that one of the most striking features of the Báb's Book, the *Bayán*, was the teaching that the believers 'must continually expect the coming of *Him whom God shall manifest*, who will confirm what he pleases of the Beyán, and alter what he pleases'. The Báb's role as a Herald is strongly evident in His teachings. He was greatly concerned that His followers should not act towards the next Prophet as, for example, the Jews acted towards Christ or the Christians towards Muḥammad. Browne writes, 'We cannot fail to be struck by the fact that when the Báb was a prisoner and an exile at Maku, probably well aware of what his ultimate fate should be, he showed far more anxiety about the reception which should be accorded to "Him whom God shall manifest" than about himself.' (Moojan Momen, ed., *Selections from the Writings of E. G. Browne on the Bábí and Bahá'í Religions*, pp. 225, 232. Originally published in the *Journal of the Royal Asiatic Society*, Oct. 1889, Art. XII, pp. 919, 926).

the way of the LORD"' (Isa. 40:3). This prophecy appears to be equally applicable to both John the Baptist (Matt. 3:3) and the Báb. Of the writings of the Báb, 'the *Bayán* (lit. Exposition) was the most holy Book of the Bábís, the Báb's followers.

In 1844, at the age of 24, the Báb (a title meaning 'Gate') proclaimed, in Shiraz, Persia, that He was a Prophet of God, founder of a new religion and forerunner of 'Him Whom God Shall Make Manifest', a title which Bahá'ís understand as a reference to Bahá'u'lláh (see *SWB* 3–5; *GPB* 25, 30). The Báb and His followers were severely persecuted, He was imprisoned and later executed in 1850.

2 Lo! He is come in the sheltering shadow of Testimony, invested with conclusive proof and evidence, and those who truly believe in Him regard His presence as the embodiment of the Kingdom of God.

3 Blessed is the man who turneth towards Him, and woe betide such as deny or doubt Him.

COMMENTARY

In these sentences Bahá'u'lláh proclaims that He is the one whom the Báb foretold would come, that the testimony of the Báb supports His claims, and that His followers, the Bahá'ís, regard closeness to Him (meaning His Cause, spirit and/or teachings) as the 'embodiment of the Kingdom of God' (*KI* 138, 142).

Bahá'u'lláh has 'come in the sheltering shadow of Testimony'. The 'Testimony' is the Báb, meaning Bahá'u'lláh has come in the shadow of the Báb's testimony, and He has come 'invested' with His own 'conclusive proof and evidence'. In His writings He asserts that the greatest proof that He is a Manifestation of God is the perfections seen in His self and His interrelated ability to impart the Word of God (GWB 49). Bahá'u'lláh argues that this is, in fact, the greatest proof that any Prophet offers (KI 91–2, 205–6, GWB 105–6).[88]

Many passages in the Bible support this point of view. The Scriptures say we are saved through faith (Eph. 2:8), but 'faith comes by hearing and hearing by the word of God' (Rom. 10:17). We must be born again (John 3:3), and Peter writes we are born again 'through the word of God' (1 Pet. 1:23). Christ came into the world to bring us into 'everlasting life', and Christ promises that 'he who hears My word and believes in Him who sent Me has everlasting life' (John 5:24). All these passages suggest that the words of the Prophets are their greatest evidence that they are truly from God. In other words, if we seek proof, we must discover whether He can impart the word of God that saves souls, gives spiritual rebirth, and bestows everlasting life.

Many people think of miracles as the proof of a Prophet.[89] Bahá'u'lláh does not refer in His writings to miracles to prove His cause. Indeed he discourages His followers from recounting miracles about Him (ESW 33). Miracles may be convincing proof to some of the people who actually see such events, but what Bahá'u'lláh wishes to direct people's attention to are proofs that are 'conclusive' (X:2). People should not have to rest their faith on events they have never seen for themselves. Instead Bahá'u'lláh offers as proof the healing power of His teachings, something that the individual can experience and know personally.

Bahá'u'lláh teaches that the miracles recorded in the Scriptures, those performed by Christ for example, actually have a spiritual significance.[90] Although the

88. See also Nabíl-i-A'ẓam, *The Dawn-Breakers*, p. 317.
89. Christ Himself indicated that miracles are not sufficient proof when He stated that false prophets are also able to work what appear to be miracles. (Matt. 24:24).
90. The Bahá'í teachings affirm that Prophets, or the Manifestations of God, as the Bahá'í writings generally refer to them, have the ability to perform miracles (SAQ ch. 22).

miracles of Christ are written in a way that appears literal, these miracles may be symbolic of how Christ healed people spiritually, bringing them back to God. Christ proclaims that His mission is to 'heal the brokenhearted' (Luke 4:18). We also know that the greatest commandment is: 'You shall love the LORD your God with all your heart, with all your soul, and all your mind' (Matt. 22:37). Christ heals those whose souls are broken-hearted over their separation from God. Through Christ the relationship between humankind and God is healed, and the love of God is restored and spread.

If the healings performed by Christ are material, then the effects must be temporary, because physical existence eventually perishes – 'flesh and blood cannot inherit the kingdom of God' (1 Cor. 15:50). But if the healings signify spiritual healing the effect may endure for ever. Therefore, from a Bahá'í point of view, there is greater significance in the miracles of Jesus if they are understood as symbols of spiritual healing.

Bahá'u'lláh writes of Christ:

> We testify that when He came into the world, He shed the splendour of His glory upon all created things. Through Him the leper recovered from the leprosy of perversity and ignorance. Through Him, the unchaste and wayward were healed. Through His power, born of Almighty God, the eyes of the blind were opened, and the soul of the sinner sanctified. Leprosy may be interpreted as any veil that interveneth between man and the recognition of the Lord, his God. Whoso alloweth himself to be shut out from Him is indeed a leper, who shall not be remembered in the Kingdom of God, the Mighty, the All-Praised. We bear witness that through the power of the Word of God every leper was cleansed, every sickness was healed, every human infirmity was banished. He it is who purified the world. Blessed is the man who, with a face beaming with light, hath turned towards Him (*GWB* 86).

XI

1 Announce thou unto the priests: Lo! He Who is the Ruler is come.
2 Step out from behind the veil in the name of thy Lord, He Who layeth low the necks of all men.
3 Proclaim then unto all mankind the glad-tidings of this mighty, this glorious Revelation.

COMMENTARY

In the preceding paragraphs Bahá'u'lláh has alluded to the testimony of biblical prophecies, the testimony of His own sacrifice, and the testimony of the Báb, in order to support His claims. Now that He has proclaimed His mission, in this paragraph Bahá'u'lláh expresses His desire that His Cause be announced to the priests. The context may suggest that He is especially calling upon converts from Christianity, the lay-persons of that Faith, to arise and accomplish this task. With the words, 'He Who is the Ruler is come', Bahá'u'lláh identifies Himself with the fulfilment of such prophecies as: 'Now out of His mouth goes a sharp sword, that with it He should strike the nations. And He Himself will rule them with a rod of iron' (Rev. 19:15).

The command to 'step out from behind the veil', means to abandon those things separating humankind from God. The words 'in the name of thy Lord' indicate that this command is in accordance with the authority given by

God. From the Bahá'í point of view, authority in spiritual matters no longer rests with the priests or clergy. In earlier times people turned to priests for guidance. This was a beneficial system because few people were literate, and the ability to study Scripture was limited. In the Bahá'í Faith there is no priesthood and Bahá'u'lláh calls on His followers to investigate the truth for themselves and take personal responsibility for proclaiming and spreading the 'glad-tidings' – or gospel – of His Cause.[91]

The Gospel of Jesus is the Revelation of Jesus. Although we may speak of four Gospels: Matthew, Mark, Luke and John, the New Testament speaks only of one Gospel. The idea of multiple Gospels would have been unknown to the Apostles. Hence the Gospel is a message rather than a specific book. The New Testament is the vehicle that preserves that message.[92] In the same way, when Bahá'u'lláh speaks of the 'glad-tidings of this mighty, this glorious Revelation' He probably intends the broad spiritual message of His Revelation.

Some Christians may object to Bahá'u'lláh's glad-tidings, citing the warning, 'even if we, or an angel from heaven, preach any other gospel to you than what we have preached to you, let him be accursed' (Gal. 1:8). Bahá'ís, however, do not regard Bahá'u'lláh's Gospel as a different Gospel in spirit: 'For the Faith of Bahá'u'lláh – if we would faithfully appraise it – can never, and in no

---

91. One of Bahá'u'lláh's tablets is specifically entitled Bishárát, meaning 'Glad-Tidings'. This tablet contains some of His basic teachings: He forbids holy war and the destruction of books, abrogates some religious practices, encourages friendly association with different religions, the study of arts and sciences, the establishment of peace and just forms of government, and so on. However, by 'glad-tidings', Bahá'u'lláh most likely intends, more broadly, the central principles of His Faith. See also footnote 51 (p. 57) for the relationship between 'glad-tidings' and 'gospel'.

92. The New Testament itself, including Paul's writings, the Qur'án, and generally the Bahá'í writings use the term in the singular form only. 'The plural form "Gospels" (Gk. euangelia) would not have been understood in the apostolic age, nor yet for two generations following; it is of the essence of the apostolic witness that there is only one true euangelion; whoever proclaims another, says Paul, is anathema (Gal. 1:8f)' (New Bible Dictionary, p. 436). See also G. Parrinder, Jesus in the Qur'án, pp. 142–51.

aspect of its teaching, be at variance, much less in conflict, with the purpose animating, or the authority invested in, the Faith of Jesus Christ' (WOB 185). Moreover, 'Abdu'l-Bahá states: 'The Cause of Bahá'u'lláh is the same as the Cause of Christ. It is the same Temple and the same foundation' (BWF 400).

It is likely that Paul's warning is directed against heretical presentations of the message of Jesus, and possibly against any spurious text that might arise in the future. It is easily arguable that Paul would not have intended his warning for the second coming of Christ Himself. This can be seen in the fact that the Old Testament also gives a similar warning forbidding any addition to the word of God, yet we have and accept the New Testament (Deut. 4:2). This indicates that it is not for people to add to the Scriptures, it is only by God's will that Scripture is revealed.

That God will reveal more is certain, for the Bible clearly prophesied that in that Day, 'He will teach us His ways' and 'out of Zion shall go forth the law' (Isa. 2:3). One interpretation of the Law anticipated in the book of Isaiah is, according to Shoghi Effendi, the very Law set out by Bahá'u'lláh in His Book, the *Kitáb-i-Aqdas* (GPB 213).

> 4 Verily, He Who is the Spirit of Truth is come to guide you unto all truth.
> 5 He speaketh not as prompted by His own self, but as bidden by Him Who is the All-knowing, the All-Wise.

COMMENTARY

Bahá'u'lláh identifies Himself here as the promised 'Spirit of Truth' who, Christ foretold, 'will guide you into all truth' (John 16:13). The words 'all truth' are not about quantitative knowledge. If they meant all knowledge, then this would mean that people would become all-knowing and there would no longer be any mysteries. Therefore, it is more probable that the truth intended involves those spiritual truths that are universal, permeating all aspects of humankind's relationship to itself, to life, and to God. A person is guided 'unto all truth' when he or she experiences the spiritual transformation that Bahá'u'lláh's Revelation effects in the believer. This transformation in itself provides the believer with direct knowledge of the truth of Bahá'u'lláh's teachings and the divine virtues underlying the spiritual life. From this point of view all the Manifestations of God, such as Christ, Muḥammad, and Bahá'u'lláh, lead their followers into all truth. Christ's prophecy, therefore, is a way of expressing that a person will know His return by His ability to bring about a spiritual transformation of the believer.

With the words, 'He speaketh not as prompted by His own self', Bahá'u'lláh affirms Christ's statement that, 'He will not speak on His own authority, but whatever He hears He will speak' (John 16:13). With these words Christ suggests that the authority of the Spirit of Truth is from God even as is His own authority: 'I have not spoken on My own authority; but the Father who sent Me gave Me a command, what I should say and what I should speak' (John 12:49). By referring to this prophecy Bahá'u'lláh is pointing out that His mission and work are not self-appointed but, rather, established on the authority of God. This is, from the Bahá'í point of view, another fulfilment of prophecy.

XII

1 Say, this is the One Who hath glorified the Son and hath exalted His Cause.

COMMENTARY

Again, Bahá'u'lláh declares that He has glorified Christ. Understanding this, one finds in His Cause the fulfilment of another of Christ's prophetic statements. Christ prophesied that 'He will glorify Me, for He will take of what is Mine and declare it to you. All things that the Father has are Mine. Therefore I said that He will take of Mine and declare it to you' (John 16:14–15).

This is perhaps one of the clearest biblical signs of the truth of Bahá'u'lláh. The New Testament gives two unmistakable criteria for discerning the spirit of God. One is set out in an Epistle by John:

> Beloved, do not believe every spirit, but test the spirits, whether they are of God; because many false prophets have gone out into the world. By this you know the Spirit of God: Every spirit that confesses that Jesus Christ has come in the flesh is of God, and every spirit that does not confess that Jesus Christ has come in the flesh is not of God' (1 John 4:1–2).

In these verses John is saying that those who confess that Jesus of Nazareth is in fact the Christ, are of God. To deny that Jesus was the Christ indicates one is not of God.

It has already been mentioned that Bahá'u'lláh affirms and teaches that Jesus is the Christ. This is so fundamental to the Bahá'í Faith that it is stated in authoritative Bahá'í writings that acceptance of Jesus Christ is an essential prerequisite of admittance into the Bahá'í Faith (*PDC* 110).

Another criterion in the New Testament is given by Paul when he writes, 'Therefore I make known to you that no one speaking by the Spirit of God calls Jesus accursed, and no one can say that Jesus is Lord except by the Holy Spirit' (1 Cor. 12:3). Bahá'u'lláh teaches that the sovereignty or lordship of the Prophets is eternal; referring to Christ, He says He is 'Lord of the visible and the invisible' (*GWB* 57) and the 'Lord of all being' (*ESW* 100). If we take these New Testament criteria as our guides, they do not alone prove that Bahá'u'lláh is a Manifestation of God, but they do demonstrate that Bahá'u'lláh's teachings about Christ support His claim to be of God and to speak by the Holy Spirit.

> 2 **Cast away, O peoples of the earth, that which ye have and take fast hold of that which ye are bidden by the All-Powerful, He Who is the Bearer of the Trust of God.**
> 3 **Purge ye your ears and set your hearts towards Him that ye may hearken to the most wondrous Call which hath been raised from Sinai, the habitation of your Lord, the Most Glorious.**
> 4 **It will, in truth, draw you nigh unto the Spot wherein ye will perceive the splendour of the light of His countenance which shineth above this luminous Horizon.**

COMMENTARY

Bahá'u'lláh invites people to investigate His Cause independently for themselves and assures them that if they do, they will find in His revelation the signs of divinity.

By the instructions to 'purge ye your ears' Bahá'u'lláh asserts that one should let go of what one has been told and investigate the truth for oneself. 'Ears' here represent one's intellectual and spiritual perception. Concerning the rejection of Prophets in former ages, Bahá'u'lláh writes:

> Unto every discerning observer it is evident and manifest that had these people in the days of each of the Manifestations of the Sun of Truth sanctified their eyes, their ears, and their hearts from whatever they had seen, heard, and felt, they surely would not have been deprived of beholding the beauty of God, nor strayed far from the habitations of glory. But having weighed the testimony of God by the standard of their own knowledge, gleaned from the teachings of the leaders of their faith, and found it at variance with their limited understanding, they arose to perpetrate such unseemly acts (KI 14–15).

This type of language is suggestive of Jesus's words: 'He who has ears to hear, let him hear!' (Matt. 11:15, 13:9, 13:43). Jesus stated:

> Therefore I speak to them in parables, because seeing they do not see, and hearing they do not hear, nor do they understand. And in them the prophecy of Isaiah is fulfilled, which says: 'Hearing you will hear and shall not understand, and seeing you will see and not perceive; for the heart of this people has grown dull. Their ears are hard of hearing, and their eyes they have closed, lest they should see with their eyes and hear with their ears, lest they should understand

with their heart and turn, so that I should heal them' (Matt. 13:13–15).

The concept of the independent investigation of truth is frequently expressed in Bahá'í writings by references to how one should avoid imitating the views of others, not knowing whether such views are correct. If people seek the truth, they should try to free themselves from preconceived ideas and influences that might interfere with their search. Addressing this subject, Bahá'u'lláh writes:

But, O my brother, when a true seeker determines to take the step of search in the path leading to the knowledge of the Ancient of Days, he must, before all else, cleanse and purify his heart, which is the seat of the revelation of the inner mysteries of God, from the obscuring dust of all acquired knowledge, and the allusions of the embodiments of satanic fancy. He must purge his breast, which is the sanctuary of the abiding love of the Beloved, of every defilement, and sanctify his soul from all that pertaineth to water and clay, from all shadowy and ephemeral attachments. He must so cleanse his heart that no remnant of either love or hate may linger therein, lest that love blindly incline him to error, or that hate repel him away from the truth (KI 192).

XIII

1 O concourse of priests!
2 Leave the bells, and come forth, then, from your churches.
3 It behoveth you, in this day, to proclaim aloud the Most Great Name among the nations.
4 Prefer ye to be silent, whilst every stone and every tree shouteth aloud: 'The Lord is come in His great glory!'?

COMMENTARY

In the previous paragraphs Bahá'u'lláh directed His call to the Christian laity. Now He specifically directs His message to the Church hierarchy, beginning with the priests, then the bishops, and finally the monks. He begins by calling priests to leave the churches and spread His Cause. Christ commanded His followers to preach the Gospel to the nations. Now Bahá'u'lláh calls upon them to 'proclaim aloud the Most Great Name among the nations', meaning they should proclaim the message and truth of Bahá'u'lláh to all people. The 'Most Great Name' is the name 'Bahá'u'lláh'.

He challenges the priests with the fact that while they have not responded, people (symbolized by the words 'stone' and 'tree') who occupy positions of lesser authority, have arisen to champion His Cause. The statement that 'every stone and every tree shouteth aloud: "The

Lord is come in His great glory!"' is a proclamation that the many prophecies which say Christ will return 'with power and great glory' have now been fulfilled (Matt. 24:30, 25:31).

The symbolism of stones and trees can be traced to the Gospel. When the disciples of Christ praised Christ openly as the King, the Gospel records that 'some of the Pharisees called to Him from the crowd, "Teacher, rebuke Your disciples." But He [Jesus] answered and said to them, "I tell you that if these should keep silent, the stones would immediately cry out"' (Luke 19:39–40).

These words from Jesus that 'the stones would immediately cry out' probably represent people, perhaps people who were regarded as especially lowly. The use of stones as a symbol for people or a person is common in the Bible. For example, Christ says, 'Therefore bear fruits worthy of repentance, and do not begin to say to yourselves, "We have Abraham as our father." For I say to you that God is able to raise up children to Abraham from these stones' (Luke 3:8). Another example is Peter's name, which means 'a stone' (John 1:42). Jesus referred to Peter saying, 'on this rock I will build My church' (Matt. 16:18).

All these examples suggest that God is able to raise up the lowly and humble to great spiritual heights. Jesus Himself is symbolized as the chief cornerstone: ' Behold, I lay in Zion a chief cornerstone, elect, precious, and he who believes on Him will by no means be put to shame' (1 Pet. 2:6; Isa. 28:16). 'The stone which the builders rejected Has become the chief cornerstone' (Ps. 118:22; 1 Pet. 2:7; also Matt. 21:42; Isa. 8:14; 1 Pet 2:8). Peter also refers to the believers as 'living stones': 'Coming to Him as to a living stone, rejected indeed by men, but chosen by God and precious, you also, as living stones, are being built up a spiritual house ' (1 Pet. 2:4–5). In a similar way, people are also symbolized as trees, judged according to their deeds or 'fruits' (Matt. 12:33–7).

Therefore it is apparent that Bahá'u'lláh is telling the priests that, while they fail to recognize His Faith, others more humble and less learned are being raised up and are championing His Cause. At the heart of this proclamation to the priests is the statement that 'The Lord is come in His great glory!'

> 5 Well is it with the man who hasteneth unto Him.
> 6 Verily, he is numbered among them whose names will be eternally recorded and who will be mentioned by the Concourse on High.[93]
> 7 Thus hath it been decreed by the Spirit in this wondrous Tablet.

COMMENTARY

Bahá'u'lláh reminds the priests of the Gospel's promises of eternal rewards. The promise of one's name being recorded in an other-worldly tablet is expressed in such biblical passages as: 'And anyone not found written in the Book of Life was cast into the lake of fire' (Rev. 20:15); 'the general assembly and the church of the firstborn who are registered in heaven' (Heb. 12:23); and 'rejoice because your names are written in heaven' (Luke 10:20). Today, He asserts, this is the reward of those who recognize Him.

The Bahá'í approach to Scripture would not support any literal interpretation that there is an actual book in another world which contains a list of names, although it can be said that such statements are meant to convey real recognition given among the believers or a general sense of spiritual reward.

---

93. The 'Concourse on High' can be understood to mean angels, that is, the souls of very devoted people.

8 He that summoneth men in My name is, verily, of Me, and he will show forth that which is beyond the power of all that are on earth.

9 Follow ye the Way of the Lord and walk not in the footsteps of them that are sunk in heedlessness.

10 Well is it with the slumberer who is stirred by the Breeze of God and ariseth from amongst the dead, directing his steps towards the Way of the Lord.

11 Verily, such a man is regarded, in the sight of God, the True One, as a jewel amongst men and is reckoned with the blissful.

COMMENTARY

Bahá'u'lláh urges the priests (and more generally, all people) to arise to teach His Faith and follow 'the Way of the Lord'. He directs them to be committed to God, not to follow the worldly and misguided, those who 'are sunk in heedlessness', and assures those who have arisen from the death of disbelief and turned towards God that they are as jewels among humankind.

He promises those who arise to teach His Faith that, in doing so, their spiritual power will overcome 'all that are on earth'. This type of promise is prophesied in the Bible concerning those who remain steadfast in the time of the end: 'And he who overcomes, and keeps My works until the end, to him I will give power over the nations' (Rev. 2:26; see also Luke 10:19). One way of understanding such promises is to view them as teachings expressing belief in the ultimate triumph of truth over falsehood, or the transcendence of spiritual qualities over worldly pursuits that perish. To have power over all that are on earth may mean to be able to persevere against temptation, to be able to see the truth despite deceptions – essentially to prevail against materialism and corruption. From this perspective it is possible to be utterly destroyed and physically killed by one's opponents and still prevail over them. Surely, nothing less than such spiritual victories have been accomplished by the Prophets, even though they be crucified or imprisoned.[94]

The 'slumberer' may be intended to represent the priests who have failed to be awakened at this, the dawn of Bahá'u'lláh's Revelation. It may also mean, more generally, the person who has allowed him or herself to drift away from the spiritual life. Bahá'u'lláh uses the phrase 'stirred by the Breeze of God'. The 'Breeze of God' signifies His Revelation. It is an apt metaphor because a breeze is a gentle wind, invisible to the eyes except for its effect on those things which it passes over. The Revelation of God is a spiritual reality which affects our souls and manifests itself visibly as it changes our lives. The word 'Breeze' appears again in verses XIV:3, XVIII:1 and XXIV:1.

By 'ariseth from amongst the dead', Bahá'u'lláh means the spiritually dead. Paul refers to the second coming of Christ in these words:

> But I do not want you to be ignorant, brethren, concerning those who have fallen asleep, lest you sorrow as others who have no hope. For if we believe that Jesus died and rose again, even so God will bring with Him those who sleep in Jesus. For this we say to you by the word of the Lord, that we who are alive and remain until the coming of the Lord will by no means precede those who are asleep. For the Lord Himself will descend from heaven with a shout, with the voice of an archangel, and with the trumpet of God. And the dead in Christ will rise first. Then we who are alive and remain shall be caught up together with them in the clouds to meet the Lord in the air. And thus we shall always be with the Lord. (1 Thess. 4:13–17).

---

94. Using the example of the Imam Husayn, Bahá'u'lláh explains that the meaning of victory over one's opponents, spoken of in the Scriptures, is spiritual (KI pp. 126–9).

Traditionally, some Christians interpret Paul's words literally, the idea being that Christians will be lifted out of their graves, made physically whole again, and will meet Christ in the sky.[95] There are many passages in the Bahá'í writings which demonstrate that Bahá'u'lláh wishes people to understand that the New Testament intends a spiritual resurrection of the dead, such as, 'The breeze of the All-Merciful hath wafted, and the souls have been quickened in the tombs of their bodies' (ESW 133), and in another passage, 'The shout hath been raised, and the people have come forth from their graves, and arising, are gazing around them. Some have made haste to attain the court of the God of Mercy, others have fallen down on their faces in the fire of Hell' (GWB 41–2).[96]

I know of no specific interpretation of 1 Thess. 4 in the authoritative Bahá'í writings. However, one possible explanation is that the dead in Christ, who will arise first, are those persons who, dissatisfied with religion, have left the Churches and largely given up belief. Today, there are many individuals who were in such a condition before recognizing Bahá'u'lláh and joining the Bahá'í community. The rest who are still alive in Christ, and who are to come next, may refer to those who never abandoned Christianity and who later recognize Bahá'u'lláh. He writes, 'O people of the Gospel! They who were not in the Kingdom have now entered it, whilst We behold you, in this day, tarrying at the gate' (PDC 106).

---

95. A literal interpretation of 1 Thess. 4:13–18 can be found in Barackman, *Practical Christian Theology*, pp. 334–6.

96. Many passages in the New Testament convey the spiritual sense of the word 'dead'. See, for example, Matt. 8:22 and James 2:26.

XIV

1 Say: In the East the Light of His Revelation hath broken; in the West the signs of His dominion have appeared.
2 Ponder this in your hearts, O people, and be not of those who grievously erred when My Remembrance came unto them at the bidding of the Almighty, the All-Praised.
3 Let the Breeze of God awaken you.
4 Verily, it hath wafted over the world.
5 Well is it with him that hath discovered the fragrance thereof and been accounted among the well-assured.

COMMENTARY

In this passage Bahá'u'lláh is saying that although His Cause began in Persia, it has now spread to the West. People should 'ponder' in their 'hearts' the significance of this and not act like those who rejected His Forerunner, 'My Remembrance', that is, the Báb. He exhorts people to let the 'Breeze of God', His Revelation, awaken them spiritually; its message has been spread over the world.

It is one of Christ's prophecies that 'For as the lightning comes from the east and flashes to the west, so also will the coming of the Son of Man be' (Matt. 24:27). It is likely that here Bahá'u'lláh is alluding to the fulfilment of this prophecy.

There are a number of possible interpretations regarding the fulfilment of this prophecy. One can, for instance, believe it refers to the speed with which the Bahá'í Faith became known to the western world through press accounts and the number of believers who appeared in countries such as England and America at the beginning of the twentieth century. In *The Revelation of Bahá'u'lláh*,[97] Adib Taherzadeh puts forward the view that 'in the West the signs of His dominion have appeared' is a reference to the establishment of the Bahá'í administrative order in Europe and, especially, America, an argument supported by the fact that this development has already occurred. He points out that Persia is regarded as the cradle of the Bahá'í Faith and America as the cradle of the Bahá'í Administrative Order. It is, perhaps, also significant that a religion often begins in one country but reaches a greater degree of establishment once it is taken to a different country.[98]

---

97. See Adib Taherzadeh, *The Revelation of Bahá'u'lláh*, vol. IV, pp. 232–3.
98. 'Abdu'l-Bahá refers to the response of the western world to the East with these words: 'The Orient has always been the center of lights. The West has acquired illumination from the East, but in some respects the reflection of the light has been greater in the Occident. This is especially true of Christianity. Christ appeared in Palestine, and His teachings were founded there. Although the doors of the Kingdom were opened in that country and the bestowals of Divinity were broadcast from its center, the people of the West have embraced and promulgated Christianity more fully than those of the East. The Sun of Reality shone forth from the horizon of the East, but its heat and ray are most resplendent in the West, where the radiant standard of Christ has been upraised. I have great hopes that the lights of Bahá'u'lláh's appearance may also find the fullest manifestation and reflection in these western regions' (PUP 289).

XV

1 O concourse of bishops!
2 Ye are the stars of the heaven of My knowledge.
3 My mercy desireth not that ye should fall upon the earth.
4 My justice, however, declareth: 'This is that which the Son hath decreed.'
5 And whatsoever hath proceeded out of His blameless, His truth-speaking, trustworthy mouth, can never be altered.

COMMENTARY

Bahá'u'lláh points out to the bishops[99] (perhaps intended to mean broadly religious leaders) that their influence and ability to lead the people is diminishing and coming to an end. He asserts that this was prophesied by Christ and therefore is irrevocable. Jesus prophesied certain signs that would accompany His future coming: 'Immediately after the tribulation of those days the sun will be darkened, and the moon will not give its light; the stars will fall from heaven, and the powers of the heavens will be shaken' (Matt. 24:29).

---

99. A bishop (Gk. episkopos) is an overseer of affairs in the Christian Church, one who is in general charge of a Church. The word implies superintendent. (See qualities and 'office of', 1 Tim. 3:1–7).

In the Kitáb-i-Íqán, Bahá'u'lláh explains that the prophecies of Christ recorded in Matthew (ch. 24) are symbolic and concern signs which take place with the appearance of all Manifestations. He discusses these prophecies in connection with Muhammad, but they are equally applicable to this age. Bahá'u'lláh explains that heaven signifies religion, and the religious leaders, such as bishops, priests, ministers and so on, are the stars of that heaven. When Christ appeared, the light of God was so bright it was like the sun during the day. After the crucifixion of Christ it was like night in comparison.[100] During the day one only needs the sun to see plainly, but at night people rely on the stars (i.e. the clergy) for direction.[101] Bahá'u'lláh says the tribulation Jesus spoke of occurs when people are unable to find the truth because of disputes, corruption, and divisions among the leaders of religion. Hence, the stars that once guided humankind can no longer be looked to for reliable guidance – they have fallen from the heaven of religion.[102]

In another tablet, Bahá'u'lláh states, concerning the Christian bishops:

> The stars of the heaven of knowledge have fallen, they that adduce the proofs they possess in order to demonstrate the truth of My Cause, and who make mention of God in My name. When I came unto them, in My majesty, however, they turned aside from Me. They, verily, are of the fallen. This is what the Spirit (Jesus) prophesied when He came with the truth' (PB 94).

It may seem strange that Bahá'u'lláh would say that the bishops 'adduce the proofs they possess in order to demonstrate' the truth of His Cause. After all, do the

---

100. Christ stated, 'As long as I am in the world, I am the light of the world' (John 9:5).
101. As in navigation, not astrology.
102. See KI, pp. 24–80.

bishops not assert proofs for Christ's Cause rather than Bahá'u'lláh's Cause? To understand Bahá'u'lláh's words it must be kept in mind that He makes no distinction between His own divine reality and the divine reality of Christ. Even as John the Baptist was the return of 'the spirit and power of Elijah' (Luke 1:17), so too Bahá'u'lláh is the return of the spirit and power of Christ – the one Christ Himself foretold would come. Thus Bahá'u'lláh says to the Christians, 'Ye make mention of Me, and know Me not.' (PB 91).

Bahá'u'lláh assures the clergy that He does not wish to see their downfall, 'My mercy desireth not . . .'. However, He points out, these are the words of Christ and as such are irrevocable: 'Heaven and earth will pass away, but My words will by no means pass away' (Luke 21:33; also Mark 13:31).[103]

6 The bells, verily, peal out My Name, and lament over Me, but My spirit rejoiceth with evident gladness.
7 The body of the Loved One yearneth for the cross, and His head is eager for the spear, in the path of the All-Merciful.
8 The ascendancy of the oppressor can in no wise deter Him from His purpose.

COMMENTARY

Bahá'u'lláh suggests here that the spirit of Christianity, symbolized by the church bells that call the believers to worship, is in harmony with His Cause – today they call out

---

103. 'Abdu'l-Bahá states: 'The traces of the spirit of Jesus Christ, the influence of his divine teaching, is present with us today, and is everlasting' (The Reality of Man, p. 20).

to the believers to come to Bahá'u'lláh; they mystically 'peal out' His name and lament over Him. He asserts His willingness to suffer as Christ did, and points out that the apparent superiority of His adversaries (or, perhaps, of all repressive regimes) is unable to frustrate God's purpose.

There may be a special significance in Bahá'u'lláh's reference to the symbols of Christ's suffering, the cross and the spear, in connection with the belief in the inability of humankind to resist God's plan. According to John, when Christ did not answer Pilate, Pilate asked, 'Are you not speaking to me? Do You not know that I have power to crucify You, and power to release You?' Christ responded: 'You could have no power at all against Me unless it had been given you from above' (John 19:10–11).

The triumph of Christ's Cause, despite persecution, is perhaps being alluded to here, in verse 8, as a testimony to or symbol of God's might and invincibility, and as an assurance of Bahá'u'lláh's own triumph.

9 We have summoned all created things to attain the presence of thy Lord, the King of all names.
10 Blessed is the man who hath set his face towards God, the Lord of the Day of Reckoning.

COMMENTARY

Despite the ascendancy of His oppressors, they have failed to prevent Bahá'u'lláh from summoning all people to 'the presence' of the Lord, 'the King of all names'. Blessed are those who have set their faces towards God, meaning they have been faithful to God. Blessed (i.e. fortunate) because God is the 'Lord of the Day of Reckoning' and has judged them to be faithful. In the New Testament, the Day of Reckoning is an anticipated final judgement by God which will accompany the return of Christ (Matt. 25:31–46; John 5:22). Bahá'u'lláh's statements suggest

COMMENTARY – XV

that the person who turns to God and acknowledges the Bahá'í Faith in this, the Day of Reckoning, will be judged by God as remaining faithful to God's word.

From the Bahá'í point of view, God's judgement can be seen in the events taking place in the world today. Notable signs of this judgement are the discrediting and fall of corrupt governments and the decline of religious orthodoxy.

In 1941, in the early part of the Second World War, Shoghi Effendi interpreted the events of our time as nothing less than the judgement of God, 'a retributory calamity and an act of holy and supreme discipline' resulting from the failure of the world to respond to Bahá'u'lláh's call (PDC 4). He said it was 'a visitation from God and a cleansing process for all mankind' that would 'punish the perversity of the human race, and weld its component parts into one organic, indivisible, world embracing community' (PDC 4). He also saw God's judgement in the decline of power and influence of those Christian ecclesiastical orders which had governed Christianity for centuries. It was his view that the leaders of the Church who 'failed to acknowledge the sovereignty of the "King of kings",' and who 'have shunned and ignored the promised Kingdom which the "Everlasting Father" has brought down from heaven, and is now establishing upon earth – these are experiencing, in this "Day of Reckoning," a crisis.' He noted the dramatic way this crisis had swept over the Church after the leaders of Christianity had failed to respond to Bahá'u'lláh. This crisis, he said, was visible in such signs as:

> The steady deterioration of their influence, the decline of their power, the damage to their prestige, the flouting of their authority, the dwindling of their congregations, the relaxation of their discipline, the restriction of their press, the timidity of their leaders, the confusion in their ranks, the progressive confiscation of their properties, the surrender of some of their most powerful strongholds, and the extinction

of other ancient and cherished institutions. Indeed, ever since the Divine summons was issued, and the invitation extended, and the warning sounded, and the condemnation pronounced, this process, that may be said to have been initiated with the collapse of the temporal sovereignty of the Roman Pontiff, soon after the Tablet to the Pope had been revealed, has been operating with increasing momentum, menacing the very basis on which the entire order is resting (PDC 103–4).[104]

Some of the specific examples of the decline of Christianity Shoghi Effendi cited were:

The wave of anticlericalism that swept over France after the collapse of the Napoleonic Empire, and which culminated in the complete separation of the Catholic Church from the state, in the laicization of the Third Republic, in the secularization of education, and in the suppression and dispersal of religious orders; the swift and sudden rise of that 'religious irreligion', that bold, conscious, and organized assault launched in Soviet Russia against the Greek Orthodox Church, that precipitated the disestablishment of the state religion, that massacred a vast number of its members originally numbering above a hundred million souls, that pulled down, closed, or converted into museums, theatres and warehouses, thousands upon thousands of churches, monasteries, synagogues and mosques, that stripped the church of its six and a half million acres of property, and sought, through its League of Militant Atheists and the promulgation of a 'five-year plan of godlessness', to loosen from its foundations the

---

104. 'In 1870, after Bahá'u'lláh had revealed His Epistle to Pope Pius IX, King Victor Emmanuel II went to war with the Papal states, and his troops entered Rome and seized it' (Shoghi Effendi, PDC p. 54). This marked the end of the Vatican's remaining temporal authority in Italy.

religious life of the masses; the dismemberment of the Austro-Hungarian Monarchy that dissolved, by one stroke, the most powerful unit which owed its allegiance to, and supported through its resources the administration of, the Church of Rome (*PDC* 104–5).

He continues to speak of 'the revolutionary movement that brought in its wake the persecution of the Catholic Church in Mexico', and other signs of decline in Western Europe and elsewhere. But he places special emphasis on the powerlessness of the Church to stop the conflict then assailing the whole world – the Second World War:

> What a sorry spectacle of impotence and disruption does this fratricidal war, which Christian nations are waging against Christian nations – Anglicans pitted against Lutherans, Catholics against Greek Orthodox, Catholics against Catholics, and Protestants against Protestants – in support of so-called Christian civilization, offer to the eyes of those who are already perceiving the bankruptcy of the institutions that claim to speak in the name, and to be the custodians, of the Faith of Jesus Christ! The powerlessness and despair of the Holy See to halt this internecine strife, in which the children of the Prince of Peace – blessed and supported by the benedictions and harangues of the prelates of a hopelessly divided church – are engaged, proclaim the degree of subservience into which the once all-powerful institutions of the Christian Faith have sunk (*PDC* 105).

XVI

1 O concourse of monks!
2 If ye choose to follow Me, I will make you heirs of My Kingdom; and if ye transgress against Me, I will, in My long-suffering, endure it patiently, and I, verily, am the Ever-Forgiving, the All-Merciful.

COMMENTARY

To be made an 'heir' is to be entitled to receive or inherit. It is one of the promises or prophecies of the Gospel that the faithful believers, the righteous, will inherit the kingdom of God: 'Then the King will say to those on His right hand, "Come, you blessed of My Father, inherit the kingdom prepared for you from the foundation of the world"' (Matt. 25:34). And in another passage: 'He who overcomes shall inherit all things, and I will be his God and he shall be My son' (Rev. 21:7). It is perhaps also worth noting that Paul warned that 'the unrighteous will not inherit the kingdom of God' (1 Cor. 6:9). Bahá'u'lláh is assuring the monks that, by recognizing Him, they will inherit the kingdom of God promised to them in the Gospel.[105]

By 'transgress against Me', Bahá'u'lláh probably does

---

105. This will be discussed further in the introduction to paragraph XXIV, pp. 154–6; see also p. 171.

not mean Himself specifically, but rather His followers or, even more broadly, any needy or oppressed person. The word 'transgress' may also have a wider meaning. It could refer to the persecution of Bahá'u'lláh's followers, the refusal to acknowledge Him, oppression of any person, or even indifference to the suffering of others.

Since this statement about transgression is in the context of the promise to make those who follow Him heirs of His Kingdom, the Gospel itself suggests that by 'transgress against Me', Bahá'u'lláh does not mean Himself. Indication of a wider meaning can be found in chapter 25 of Matthew.[106] There Christ's return is described: The 'Son of Man comes in His glory', gathers the nations before Him and 'as a shepherd divides His sheep from the goats' (Matt. 25:31–2). 'Then the King' says to His sheep (i.e. 'the righteous' v. 37):

> 'Come, you blessed of My Father, inherit the kingdom prepared for you from the foundation of the world: for I was hungry and you gave Me food; I was thirsty and you gave Me drink; I was a stranger and you took Me in; I was naked and you clothed Me; I was sick and you visited Me; I was in prison and you came to Me.' Then the righteous will answer Him, saying, 'Lord, when did we see You hungry and feed You, or thirsty and give You drink?' . . . And the King will answer and say to them, 'Assuredly, I say to you, inasmuch as you did it to one of the least of these My brethren, you did it to Me' (Matt. 25:34–40).

Christ's words here make a clear link between kindness to the needy and kindness to Him. The 'kingdom' is the reward of those who perform this kindness (Matt. 25:34). In verses 41–6 Christ goes on to link indifference to the needy with indifference to Him. Those who fail to care for

---

106. A wide interpretation of Bahá'u'lláh's references to Himself will also be discussed in the commentary on verse XXIV:16, pp. 179–80.

the needy are made to 'depart' into 'everlasting fire' (Matt. 25:41; also 25:46).

Since the Kingdom Bahá'u'lláh speaks of is the same as that referred to in Matthew, it seems likely that the type of unrighteousness Christ spoke of is also found in the meaning of Bahá'u'lláh's words 'if ye transgress against Me'. However, there is a difference between Jesus's words, where the transgressors will find themselves in 'everlasting fire', and Bahá'u'lláh's words, as He states that He will 'endure it patiently'. This difference is not a contradiction but rather an indication of two related truths. Christ's words about punishment affirm the spiritual deprivation that results from unrighteousness. On the other hand, Bahá'u'lláh's words do not cancel out the truth of what Christ said but express Bahá'u'lláh's attitude towards those who persecute His followers, do not accept His Faith, and are not responsive to those in need.

Bahá'u'lláh teaches that His followers should not use violence to resist opposition to His Cause. 'Abdu'l-Bahá stated:

> Bahá'u'lláh proclaimed that, inasmuch as God is the one heavenly Shepherd and all mankind are the sheep of His fold, the religion or guidance of God must be the means of love and fellowship in the world. If religion proves to be the source of hatred, enmity and contention, if it becomes the cause of warfare and strife and influences men to kill each other, its absence is preferable. For that which is productive of hatred amongst the people is rejected by God, and that which establishes fellowship is beloved and sanctioned by Him. Religion and divine teachings are like unto a remedy. A remedy must produce the condition of health. If it occasions sickness, it is wiser and better to have no remedy whatever. This is the significance of the statement that if religion becomes the cause of warfare and bloodshed, irreligion and the absence of religion are preferable among mankind (*PUP* 298).

Bahá'u'lláh also teaches that His followers should not quarrel with those who do not accept His religion. He says, 'O people! Consort with the followers of all religions in a spirit of friendliness and fellowship' (TB 22).[107] Bahá'u'lláh's teachings acknowledge the individual rights of different religious communities, advocate reverence for their Scriptures and places of worship, and forbid the use of coercion to spread His cause.

Finally, in relation to Christ's words about the needy, Bahá'u'lláh teaches that people who do not respond to the poor should not be forced to be charitable. 'Abdu'l-Bahá writes:

> To state the matter briefly, the Teachings of Bahá'u'lláh advocate voluntary sharing, and this is a greater thing than the equalization of wealth. For equalization must be imposed from without, while sharing is a matter of free choice.
>
> Man reacheth perfection through good deeds, voluntarily performed, not through good deeds the doing of which was forced upon him. And sharing is a personally chosen righteous act: that is, the rich should extend assistance to the poor, they should expend their substance for the poor, but of their own free will, and not because the poor have gained this end by force. For the harvest of force is turmoil and the ruin of the social order. On the other hand voluntary sharing, the freely-chosen expending of one's substance, leadeth to society's comfort and

---

107. Many religions have, at different times in history, suffered persecution from the followers of other religions. Jews, for example, have suffered the intolerances of both Christians and Muslims. Bahá'u'lláh teaches that such persecution is unjust and must not be allowed. In 1912 'Abdu'l-Bahá related that: 'At that time the Jews were greatly oppressed in Persia. Bahá'u'lláh especially recommended justice for them, saying that all are the servants of God, and in the eye of the government they should be equally estimated. If justice is not dealt out, if these oppressions are not removed and if thou dost not obey God, the foundations of thy government will be razed.' The Sháh did not answer this Epistle of the Blessed Perfection [Bahá'u'lláh]. Then God destroyed the foundations of his sovereignty' (PUP p. 223).

peace. It lighteth up the world; it bestoweth honour upon humankind (SWA 115; see also 302).

All these points concerning the peaceful purpose of religion, religious tolerance, and non-coercion with regard to spirituality are embraced in His statement, 'if ye transgress against Me, I will, in My long-suffering, endure it patiently'.

In paragraphs XIII–XVI, Bahá'u'lláh has specifically called upon the ecclesiastical leaders of Christianity. In the next paragraph, Bahá'u'lláh calls out to Syria, a land with a rich religious history.

XVII

1 O land of Syria!
2 What hath become of thy righteousness?
3 Thou art, in truth, ennobled by the footsteps of thy Lord.
4 Hast thou perceived the fragrance of heavenly reunion, or art thou to be accounted of the heedless?

COMMENTARY

The thrust of this paragraph, referring to Syria, seems to be an announcement that Bahá'u'lláh has re-established the ancient and eternal Faith of God.

Syria was the name of Israel at the time of Christ (Matt. 4:24). The 'righteousness' of Syria may refer to times in the past when people who inhabited that land were faithful to God's covenant. By 'ennobled by the footsteps of thy Lord' He may mean Christ, or Himself, or possibly both. 'Heavenly reunion' suggests that Bahá'u'lláh's exile to Syria, the land of Christ, has, in fact, brought the Spirit of Christ back to the place of Christianity's birth. The 'fragrance of heavenly reunion' may be a way of suggesting the signs of spirituality among His followers.[108] To

---

108. Cf. XIV:5; XVIII:4; XIX:3, 6; XXIV:11.

attain this 'reunion' is to attain the Kingdom of God, or the state of heaven (*ESW* 132).[109]

In the present context of verses XVII:1–4, it seems reasonable to speculate that 'reunion' could involve the return of God's Faith to Syria, but there are many times when Bahá'u'lláh uses the word 'reunion' as the goal attained by the individual seeker (e.g. *KI* 61, 201, 255). The word may relate to the fact that humankind is created by God but subsequently strays from God's will. God then sends Prophets to call humankind back to God. In this way humankind is reunited with God. The word 'reunion' is used in a similar way with reference to Christ in verse IV:2 and appears again in verse XXIV:11. Bahá'u'lláh first makes reference to Syria. In the next paragraph He directs attention more specifically to Bethlehem.

---

109. There may be a relationship between repentance and reunion. In the Old Testament 'the idea of repentance is often expressed by such words as "turn", "return". The fundamental idea behind the use of these words in a religious sense is that of subjects who had rebelled coming back to serve their rightful king.' (Alan Richardson, ed., *A Theological Word Book of the Bible*, p. 191).

XVIII

1 Bethlehem is astir with the Breeze of God.
2 We hear her voice saying: 'O most generous Lord!
3 Where is Thy great glory established?
4 The sweet savours of Thy presence have quickened me, after I had melted in my separation from Thee.
5 Praised be Thou in that Thou hast raised the veils, and come with power in evident glory.'
6 We called unto her from behind the Tabernacle of Majesty and Grandeur: 'O Bethlehem!
7 This Light hath risen in the orient, and travelled towards the occident, until it reached thee in the evening of its life.

COMMENTARY

In these verses, Bahá'u'lláh writes a kind of mystical dialogue between Himself and Bethlehem, the place of Jesus's birth. It is difficult to interpret such symbolic language. What this dialogue may be saying is that the Spirit of Christ (i.e. Bahá'u'lláh) has returned to revive the original Christianity established by Christ. The spirit of Christianity is quickened or reawakened by the life of Bahá'u'lláh following its decline over the centuries. Bahá'u'lláh has removed the barriers separating people from God and is calling out to true Christianity, announcing His advent.

This interpretation is simply based on the assumed meanings given to the symbolic words. Bethlehem, for instance, may represent the original spirit of Christianity. The word Bethlehem literally means 'house of bread'. Jesus is the 'bread which came down from heaven' (John 6:41). Also, the word 'house' has a wide meaning in Hebrew usage, frequently referring to the family or a whole people. This meaning is carried over to the New Testament, where the church is referred to as the 'members of the household of God' (Eph. 2:19). The believers are the living stones that make up a 'spiritual house' (1 Pet. 2:5). Therefore, Bethlehem may signify the house of bread, the faithful believers of the Revelation and Cause of Christ. Perhaps Bethlehem symbolizes Christians who have accepted the Revelation of Bahá'u'lláh.

Bethlehem addresses Bahá'u'lláh: 'Where is Thy great glory established?' This may be a way of conveying that the spirit of Christianity testifies to or wishes to hasten to Bahá'u'lláh. The 'sweet savours of Thy presence' may signify Bahá'u'lláh's appearance, His renunciation, and the divine virtues which have 'quickened' the spirit of Christianity after it had 'melted' over the centuries through separation from the spirit of Christ.

Bethlehem acknowledges Bahá'u'lláh's glory, proclaiming that He has 'come with power in evident glory'. The words 'power in evident glory' give emphasis to the claim that the prophecy of Christ's return 'with power and great glory' (Matt. 24:30, 25:31) has been fulfilled in such a way that it is 'evident'. It is evident in that His sacrifice reveals His 'power and great glory'. This is an extremely important point because Christ's return in glory is a theme which is central to the prophecies of the Old Testament (e.g. Ezek. 43:2; Isa. 35:2, 40:5), and the prophecies of the New Testament (e.g. Mark 8:38, 13:26; Rev. 21:23). It is also central to Bahá'u'lláh's claims. As we have seen, Bahá'u'lláh proclaims in the very first sentence of this tablet that He has come 'invested with transcendent glory', and in the opening verses He goes on to assert that He has come 'from the heaven of eternity in His great glory' (III:4). It is so central a characteristic that even His name, as was noted in the commentary on verse III:2, means 'The Glory of God'. The relationship of this important theme of the glory of Bahá'u'lláh to His sacrifice has already been discussed in the commentary on verse VI:2, and will be taken up again in the commentary on verses XX:1–5.

Bahá'u'lláh says 'We[110] called' Bethlehem, that is Christianity, 'from behind the Tabernacle of Majesty and Grandeur'. This may be a way of saying that Bahá'u'lláh is calling Christians to God in a manner that reflects or testifies to the majesty and grandeur of God. The Tabernacle may be used here by Bahá'u'lláh as a symbol of a place of God's presence. He thus calls out from God's presence, or with the authority of God.[111]

Like Christ (John 9:5), Bahá'u'lláh characterizes Himself as a 'Light'. He says the Light has 'risen in the orient', meaning He has come from Persia, and 'travelled towards the occident', when, as the result of exile, He was forced West to imprisonment in 'Syria' (then Palestine, part of the Ottoman Empire, now Israel). The 'evening of its life' may mean the last years of Bahá'u'lláh's physical life.

---

110. In a letter on this subject, Stephen Lambden commented: 'In saying that "We called unto her [Bethlehem] from behind the Tabernacle of Majesty and Grandeur" Bahá'u'lláh seems to be expressing the fact that the voice of God was heard through Himself (thus, "We") from a lofty place in the spiritual world.'

111. The words 'behind the Tabernacle' should not be taken in a literal geographical sense. Taking into consideration the comments of several Bahá'í scholars who were familiar with the original Arabic, it seems more reasonable to interpret this phrase as a way of suggesting the specific context, i.e. Majesty and Grandeur, from which the Revelation of Bahá'u'lláh is addressed mystically to Bethlehem.

8 Tell Me then: Do the sons recognize the Father, and acknowledge Him, or do they deny Him, even as the people aforetime denied Him (Jesus)?'
9 Whereupon she cried out saying: 'Thou art, in truth, the All-Knowing, the Best-Informed.'

COMMENTARY

Here, continuing the dialogue with Bethlehem (XVIII:1), Bahá'u'lláh asks, do Christians recognize Him or have they responded as the Jews did to Christ?

The 'sons' signify the followers of Christ. John wrote: 'But as many as received Him, to them He gave the right to become children of God, even to those who believe in His name: who were born, not of blood, nor of the will of the flesh, nor of the will of man, but of God' (John 1:12–13; see also Rom. 8:14). When Bahá'u'lláh asks, 'do they recognize the Father', He is referring to Himself, either as the Father foretold in Isaiah (9:6), or as One who is a Manifestation of God the Father. However, such a distinction may be superfluous, even as indicated in the words of Christ: 'If you had known Me, you would have known My Father also; and from now on you know Him and have seen Him' (John 14:7; see also KI 178).

10 Verily, We behold all created things moved to bear witness unto Us.
11 Some know Us and bear witness, while the majority bear witness, yet know Us not.

COMMENTARY

'Some know Us and bear witness' may be referring to the believers, the Bahá'ís. 'While the majority bear witness, yet know Us not' may mean the unbelievers. But how do the unbelievers bear witness? This commentary will consider several possible interpretations. The first involves speculation in the area of what some theologians call natural or general revelation. Revelation through the Prophets is sometimes called special Revelation, while the revelation of God in the universe and world around us is called general revelation (Rom. 1:19–20; KI 103–4).[112]

All things reflect to some measure the attributes of God. Furthermore, God operates in the world, even outside the community of believers. One can argue that God's grace, judgement and plan can be seen in many things occurring in the world that Bahá'ís have little influence over. Bahá'í writings assert that the calamities afflicting the world today will help lead humanity towards a world order such as envisioned by Bahá'u'lláh (WOB 34, 43, 45, 202).[113] Currently it can also be argued that throughout the world people who are not Bahá'ís have gradually come to accept many of Bahá'u'lláh's teachings, such as the need to eliminate religious, racial and gender prejudices, the need for an international language, even a world tribunal; thus they know Him not, yet 'bear witness'. This type of reasoning rests on the concept of divine providence or active participation of God in the world, and involves the distinction between general and special revelation described above.

A second interpretation of 'We behold all created things moved to bear witness unto Us' may be arrived at by a more precise understanding of 'all created things'. 'All created things' may not mean literally all things, both material and spiritual. It may also mean only those persons who are 'created' in the sense of a new and spiritual creation (Rev. 21:3–5; 2 Tim. 1:10). Therefore

---

112. See Barackman, Practical Christian Theology, pp. 21–2.

113. Gibbon notes that while the Christians struggled to spread the Gospel, circumstances outside their control worked in their favour. For example: 'The public highways, which had been constructed for the use of the legions, opened an easy passage for the Christian missionaries from Damascus to Corinth, and from Italy to the extremity of Spain or Britain' (Decline and Fall of the Roman Empire, p. 182).

the Christian or any truly devoted follower of one of the world's great religions, who bears witness to that religion, is in effect bearing witness to the same truth that is now manifested in the Bahá'í Faith. All religions possess the same light even though outwardly they have different names. This suggests that Bahá'u'lláh is saying that the Bahá'ís 'know Us and bear witness, while the majority' of the religious people 'bear witness, yet know Us not'.

If it seems implausible to view 'all created things' as referring only to religious persons, the spiritually reborn, then consider similar verses in Scripture. For example, Paul says the Gospel has gone out to 'all the world' and that it 'was preached to every creature under heaven' (Col. 1:6, 23). These verses are thought to have been written around AD 60. If we take them to mean literally all creatures – people, animals and so on – it is extremely difficult to imagine how they could be true. On the other hand, if viewed from a spiritual standpoint, it is not difficult. Obviously Paul was concerned with spiritual life, the 'new creation' (2 Cor. 5:17). Moreover, if we take into consideration Bahá'u'lláh's explanations of the word 'heaven', we find additional reason to understand Paul's words in a purely spiritual context (KI 44). Every 'creature under heaven' could mean that every believer in Christ – that is, under the heaven of His Revelation – has been preached to and has heard the Gospel.

XIX

1 Mount Sinai is astir with the joy of beholding Our countenance.
2 She hath lifted her enthralling voice in glorification of her Lord, saying: 'O Lord!
3 I sense the fragrance of Thy garment.
4 Methinks Thou art near, invested with the signs of God.
5 Thou hast ennobled these regions with Thy footsteps.
6 Great is the blessedness of Thy people, could they but know Thee and inhale Thy sweet savours; and woe betide them that are fast asleep.'

COMMENTARY

Once more Bahá'u'lláh speaks in the form of a dialogue, this time between Mount Sinai and Himself. As noted before, such rhapsodic language defies any confident interpretation. However, one meaning that may be at the heart of these verses is the covenant of God. The following speculation is based on that assumption.

God has established and, throughout the ages, has renewed His covenant with humankind. That covenant essentially is the agreement or understanding that God guides and delivers humanity from evil and, in return, humankind must faithfully serve God. Bahá'u'lláh expresses in symbolic language how this ancient covenant foreshadows or testifies to His Revelation, which has renewed and ennobled the covenant. Yet He waits for the Jews, Christians, and other upholders of these earlier covenants to recognize that He has offered Himself up to God to re-establish that eternal covenant. Finally, He says that sorrow will befall those who are without faith, perhaps, in this context, outside the covenant of God.

It is difficult to narrow these verses down to a definitive interpretation, but this is how the above understanding was reached. Bahá'u'lláh may be suggesting that the ancient covenant of God, symbolized by Mount Sinai (Gal. 4:24–6) is astir with the Revelation of God, signified by 'our countenance'.[114] The covenant of God (i.e. Mount Sinai) senses the divinity and greatness (i.e. fragrance) of His Cause, symbolized as His 'garment'. The religion of God is likened to a garment in the Gospel as well (Matt. 9:16; Mark 2:21). Symbolically this covenant testifies to 'the signs of God' in Bahá'u'lláh's Revelation. 'Thou hast ennobled these regions' may refer to the covenant itself being strengthened through Bahá'u'lláh's Revelation.[115] 'Great is the blessedness of Thy people'[116] may signify the believers of former religions, 'could they but know Thee and inhale Thy sweet savours', meaning if these people could only appreciate how Bahá'u'lláh has offered Himself as a sacrifice to God on behalf of humankind. The words 'inhale Thy sweet savours' may be an allusion to the ancient practice of burning an animal sacrifice on an altar, 'as an offering made by fire, a sweet aroma [or 'sweet savour', KJV] to the Lord' (Lev. 1:9, 13, 17; Exod. 40:27).[117] This perhaps suggests that He has offered

---

114. The passage calls to mind the expressive language of Ps. 68:8: 'Sinai itself was moved at the presence of God.'

115. See XXIV:20.

116. 'Thy people' may actually refer to those followers of Bahá'u'lláh who were unable to meet Him because He was imprisoned.

117. The term 'savours' is frequently found in the Bible. It is rooted in the Old Testament but is used symbolically in the New Testament, where it comes from the word 'euodia', meaning 'fragrance'. W. E. Vine writes that it 'is used metaphorically (a) of those who in the testimony of the gospel are to God "a sweet savour of Christ", 2 Cor. 2:15; (b) of the giving up of His life by Christ for

Himself as a sacrifice for the establishment of the covenant of God. The warning 'woe betide them that are fast asleep' refers to those who are without faith.

---

us, an offering and a sacrifice to God for an odor . . . of "a sweet smell", Eph. 5:2, RV (KJV, 'a sweet smelling [savour]'); (c) of material assistance sent to Paul from the church at Philippi "[an odor] of a sweet smell", Phil. 4:18. In all three instances the fragrance is that which ascends to God through the person, and as a result of the sacrifice, of Christ' Vine's Expository Dictionary of Biblical Words, p. 548). This practice is carried out in many religions today with incense, a gum or spice which when burned gives off a sweet savour.

XX

1 Happy art thou who hast turned thy face towards My countenance, inasmuch as thou hast rent the veils asunder, hast shattered the idols and recognized thine eternal Lord.

COMMENTARY

At the beginning of the *Lawḥ-i-Aqdas*, Bahá'u'lláh directed His words to a specific unnamed believer. Then He turned His attention to Christians in general. Now with this paragraph (XX) Bahá'u'lláh begins a transition. The remainder of this tablet is once again directed to the individual believer in His Cause.

In this passage (XX:1) Bahá'u'lláh gives an assurance that the person who overcomes his or her errors and doubts and recognizes His station, will obtain happiness.

For most people, belief in Bahá'u'lláh must, of necessity, entail a fundamental break with some traditional or conventional views. In order to become a believer, the seeker must overcome whatever has prevented others from accepting Bahá'u'lláh's teachings. This break with accepted norms which are contrary to Bahá'u'lláh's Revelation, and the overcoming of doubts, can be likened to the rending of veils and shattering of idols.

Some things which can be represented as veils that come between people and their recognition of Bahá'u'lláh might be His human qualities, such as His need to eat or sleep, His name or nationality, or His physical death.[118] Another veil might be the way in which many people expect the literal fulfilment of certain prophecies which have not come to pass. Some of His teachings and laws or the shortcomings of His followers could also be as veils to some people, preventing them from accepting His Cause.

In Bahá'u'lláh's other writings the symbolism of the veil is often accompanied by fuller elaboration. For example, He speaks of the veils of glory, the veils of learning, the veils of limitation, and so on (KI 155, 164–87, 214). These phrases suggest metaphors for material attachments or beliefs. Such veils may also represent aspirations for such things as leadership or wealth or anything which, in effect, prevents one from recognizing God's Messengers or the truth.

The term 'veils' has been used as a symbol from early biblical times, and appears in the New Testament, Islamic tradition, and the Bahá'í Faith. The metaphor of veils for those things which come between humankind and the recognition of God or God's Messengers is found in an Islamic tradition which Bahá'u'lláh cites in His Book, the Kitáb-i-Íqán (164, 188). This metaphor is the symbolic equivalent to the veil in the Tabernacle mentioned in the Bible (Exod. 26). The Old Testament records that this veil was used as a partition to separate the people from the innermost chamber of the Tabernacle containing the 'Holy of Holies'.[119] Only the high priest was allowed to go behind this veil into the chamber.

It is also recorded that, after Moses had spoken with God on Mount Sinai, 'the skin of his face shone ... So when Aaron and all the children of Israel saw Moses, behold, the skin of his face shone, and they were afraid to come near him' (Exod. 34:29–30). For this reason Moses 'put a veil on his face' (Exod. 34:33). St Paul used the veil as a metaphor for the inability of the Jewish people to understand the relationship of the Old Testament to the

---

118. For an example concerning Christ see Matt. 11:19.
119. The Ark of the Covenant, containing the Tablets of the Law.

appearance of Jesus Christ: 'For until this day the same veil remains unlifted in the reading of the Old Testament, because the veil is taken away in Christ. But even to this day, when Moses is read, a veil lies on their hearts. Nevertheless when one turns to the Lord, the veil is taken away' (2 Cor. 3:14–15). Thus, in the New Testament, the veil is used as a symbol which represents something that prevents a person from seeing the truth.

This also gives us a strong reason to believe that a symbolic meaning was intended when the veil of the Temple was mentioned in connection with the death of Christ. According to the Gospel, when Christ died on the Cross, 'the veil of the Temple was torn in two from top to bottom' (Mark 15:38). The rending of the veil may mean that Jesus's death on the Cross revealed 'the power of God and the wisdom of God' so that all who believed could see it for themselves (1 Cor. 1:22–5).

In a similar way, Bahá'u'lláh asserts that God's glory is revealed through His Cause 'without veil or concealment' in this age:

> Every discerning eye can, in this Day, perceive the dawning light of God's Revelation, and every attentive ear can recognize the Voice that was heard from the Burning Bush. Such is the rushing of the waters of Divine mercy, that He Who is the Day Spring of the signs of God and the Revealer of the evidences of His glory is without veil or concealment associating and conversing with the peoples of the earth and its kindreds (GWB 271).

Bahá'u'lláh is, in effect, proclaiming that He has unveiled the glory of God through His Revelation. He is asserting that, through belief in Him, a person can perceive spiritual truths that are otherwise veiled to those who are not believers. In the next four paragraphs Bahá'u'lláh challenges those Christians whose 'veils' have prevented them from believing in Him.

Similar to the symbolism of the veil, a person's adherence to an egotistical nationalism, to racism, to a materialistic lifestyle, or to anything that claims the loyalty which belongs to God alone (Isa. 42:8), can be likened to an 'idol' that must be 'shattered', renounced, and overcome in order to follow Bahá'u'lláh's teachings. This liberation from the misconceptions that are the sources of so much hatred and unhappiness in the world on the one hand, and the new life of faith on the other hand, naturally inspires happiness for the believer.

The concept of idolatry gradually evolves in the Bible to take on a broader meaning. In the Hebrew Scriptures, idolatry is seen in the form of a materialistic religious consciousness and practice. Most notably, this takes place when the Jews turn away from God to worship the golden calf (Exod. 32). In response, Moses and the Prophets who came after Him tried to deliver the people from such practices and to guide them to belief in one God who is transcendent and spiritual in nature. Isaiah taught that the worship of idols is a delusion (Isa. 44:20) and causes spiritual blindness (Isa. 44:18).

The meaning of involvement in idolatry becomes broader in the New Testament message, where idolatry is associated with sin (Gal. 5:19–20) and covetousness (1 Cor. 5:11; Eph. 5:5; Col. 3:5). This evolution towards a more clearly stated concept of idolatry, as being any orientation that diverts a person from God, continues in the Bahá'í Faith. In Bahá'u'lláh's writings, He speaks of 'idols of vain imaginings and corrupt desires', 'idols of imitation', and 'idols of superstition'.

Bahá'u'lláh writes:

> People for the most part delight in superstitions. They regard a single drop of the sea of delusion as preferable to an ocean of certitude. By holding fast unto names they deprive themselves of the inner reality and by clinging to vain imaginings they are kept back from the Dayspring of heavenly signs. God grant you may be graciously aided under all conditions to shatter the idols of superstition and to tear

away the veils of the imaginations of men. Authority lieth in the grasp of God, the Fountainhead of revelation and inspiration and the Lord of the Day of Resurrection (TB 58).[120]

2 The people of the Qur'án have risen up against Us without any clear proof or evidence, tormenting Us at every moment with a fresh torment.
3 They idly imagine that tribulations can frustrate Our Purpose.
4 Vain indeed is that which they have imagined.
5 Verily, thy Lord is the One Who ordaineth whatsoever He pleaseth.

COMMENTARY

In this passage Bahá'u'lláh refers to the fact that the followers of Islam have persecuted Him. He refers to Muslims who, like Christians, are divided into many sects, with the all inclusive words 'the people of the Qur'án'. The Bahá'í Faith recognizes the divine inspiration and authenticity of the Qur'án, Islam's holy Book.

Bahá'u'lláh asserts that His persecutors have no 'clear proof or evidence', meaning that He is innocent of any wrongdoing and that their opposition is without scriptural justification. He points out that they have deluded themselves in thinking that by persecuting His cause they can stop its progress. Bahá'u'lláh conveys the conviction that, because His Cause is ordained by God, its fate rests with God alone, and humankind cannot resist or thwart God's plan.

---

120. Gibbon writes: 'A state of scepticism and suspense may amuse a few inquisitive minds. But the practice of superstition is so congenial to the multitude that, if they are forcibly awakened, they still regret the loss of their pleasing vision' (*The Decline and Fall of the Roman Empire*, p. 181).

COMMENTARY – XX

It seems unlikely that the Muslims who opposed Bahá'u'lláh thought they were trying to eradicate a Faith that was truly from God. Nevertheless, their guilt lies in their narrow-minded refusal to investigate His Cause, the insincerity of their own faith, and the brutality with which they persecuted His followers, a brutality and cruelty that offends the conscience of every just person. They were too arrogant to consider fairly Bahá'u'lláh's own virtues, His open recognition of their Faith, (the Faith of Islam) and the inspiration of His teachings. Like the religious authorities at the time of Christ, they took away the 'key of knowledge', did not enter in themselves, and those who were entering they hindered (Luke 11:52, Matt. 23:13).

Because the Bahá'í Faith originated in Persia (Iran), where the government was (and is) shaped by the practices and beliefs of Islam, it was the leaders of that system of religious belief who felt themselves challenged and who, therefore, arose to suppress the Bahá'ís. The most severe opposition occurred during the time of the Báb. The scholar Bausani writes:

> If this movement had taken hold, it would have destroyed the privileges of the Shi'ite[121] clergy and would have had a definitely beneficial influence on the life of the country, but it was bitterly opposed by both the religious and political authorities. Thousands were martyred for supporting the new faith, and Renan later compared its beginnings with those of the early Christians.[122]

Following persecutions in 1852, Bahá'u'lláh was exiled to Baghdad, never to return to Persia. Throughout Bahá'u'lláh's life, His exiles and imprisonments were under the order of Islamic governments. Even in recent times this persecution of Bahá'ís by 'the people of the

---
121. Shi'ite or Shi'ih Islam is one of the two primary divisions of Islam.
122. Alessandro Bausani, *The Persians*, p. 166.

Qur'án' has continued. Iranian Bahá'ís suffered attacks in 1955, 1963, and when the so-called 'Islamic Revolution' took place in the late 1970s and throughout the 1980s.

The effort to persecute or destroy God's plan fails largely because persecution facilitates the consequent sacrifice of the Messenger of God. The willingness to suffer helps reveal such divine qualities as love and devotion, and people of pure heart are drawn to this testimony. To those who believe, this sacrifice becomes a sign of God's might, power, and transcendence. Persecution does not refute truth, it only reveals the innocence of the oppressed and the tyranny of the oppressors. E. G. Browne writes that the Bábí Faith underwent a 'baptism of blood which was the terror and wonder even of those who proscribed and persecuted it'.[123]

The futility of persecution is evident in the suffering and sacrifice of Christ. The Bible suggests that this suffering is not a humiliation nor is it a sign of powerlessness, but that to the spiritually-minded this suffering reveals the power and glory of Christ. Paul writes, 'For Jews request a sign, and Greeks seek after wisdom; but we preach Christ crucified, to the Jews a stumbling block and to the Greeks foolishness, but to those who are called, both Jews and Greeks, Christ the power of God and the wisdom of God' (1 Cor. 1:22–4). Another passage which affirms this understanding can be found in the Book of Revelation: 'Worthy is the Lamb who was slain to receive power and riches and wisdom, and strength and honour and glory and blessing!' (Rev. 5:12). This message is apparent in Bahá'u'lláh's words concerning His oppressors, 'They are, however, oblivious of the fact that abasement in the path of God is My true glory' (ESW 125). Therefore, the Christian who looks for the glory of Christ's return should not look for temporal victory but should, rather, look to the glory revealed in the suffering and imprisonment of Bahá'u'lláh!

---

123. Moojan Momen, ed., *Selections from the Writings of E. G. Browne on the Bábí and Bahá'í Religions*, p. 407.

XXI

1 I never passed a tree but Mine heart addressed it saying: 'O would that thou wert cut down in My Name, and My body crucified upon thee.'
2 We revealed this passage in the Epistle to the Sháh that it might serve as a warning to the followers of religions.
3 Verily, thy Lord is the All-Knowing, the All-Wise.

COMMENTARY

In this passage Bahá'u'lláh expresses His continual willingness to suffer for the sake of establishing the Cause of God. He conveyed this to the ruler of Persia (Iran).[124] But, interestingly, the message is apparently not to the Sháh alone but is directed as a warning to 'the followers of religions'.

In what way is this a warning to the religious? Is this a warning in the sense of a testimony to those who would profess religion that they too must sacrifice – a taking up of the Cross? (Matt. 10:38). More probably the use of the Crucifixion is a symbolic way of associating the triumph

---

124. The tablet Bahá'u'lláh refers to is *Lawḥ-i-Sulṭán*, the tablet to Náṣiri'd-Dín Sháh, revealed to Adrianople, 1863–8 (Shoghi Effendi, *PDC* 40; see also Adib Taherzadeh, *The Revelation of Bahá'u'lláh*, vol. II, pp. 337–57). Náṣiri'd-Dín Sháh reigned from 1848 until he was assassinated in 1896 by a follower of Jamálu'd-Dín-i-Afghání.

of Christianity, despite persecution, with His own suffering. Thus it is a warning directed at the followers of religions who might assume the role of persecutors – that is, the cause of Bahá'u'lláh, like that of Christ, is invincible to their attacks. If they had tried to force Bahá'u'lláh to recant, they would have failed because He was willing to die. And if they killed Him it would only have added to the force of His testimony, even as His exiles and imprisonments added to the testimony of His Cause.

XXII

1 Let not the things they have perpetrated grieve thee.
2 Truly they are even as dead, and not living.
3 Leave them unto the dead, then turn thy face towards Him Who is the Life-Giver of the world.

COMMENTARY

Throughout this tablet Bahá'u'lláh has referred repeatedly to the persecution He has had to suffer. However, His intention is not to make people feel sorry for Him. This is evident in the words, 'Let not the things they have perpetrated grieve thee.' But it raises the question, why then does Bahá'u'lláh draw attention to His own suffering? There are two important reasons. The first concerns the significance of His sacrifices as a testimony to the world of His sincerity, steadfastness, and conviction. This has already been mentioned in the commentary to verse VI:2 (see p. 58–60). The second reason is that His life serves as a sign to the world revealing the meaning of true glory. It is not Bahá'u'lláh's wish that the acts committed against Him should cause sadness. Rather, He wants the world to discover the significance of why He was willing to make the sacrifices that He did. His life reveals that real glory is not as many people imagine it; it does not depend on material property, the support of popular opinion or temporal victories. Real glory is revealed in the triumph of the spiritual life. It is a glory attainable even though one may be among the poorest of the poor or one who is, to all outward appearance, defeated even to the point of death.

Bahá'u'lláh's persecutors were both wealthy and powerful, yet He characterizes them as those who 'are even as the dead'. He counsels people to disassociate themselves from their hostile or indifferent ways and turn instead to faith in Him. Faith is the essence of spiritual life. Thus Bahá'u'lláh refers to Himself as the 'Life-Giver of the world'.

There can be no doubt that Bahá'u'lláh wishes to recall the words of Christ. The words follow closely those of the Gospel. A disciple chose to follow Christ but hesitated, saying, '"Lord, let me first go and bury my father." But Jesus said to him, "Follow Me, and let the dead bury their own dead"' (Matt. 8:21–2). Christ characterizes the disbelievers as those who are like the dead.

True life is spiritual life, the life of faith, and death is disbelief and the absence of spiritual life. The call to follow Bahá'u'lláh means taking up the life of faith. It is probable that Bahá'u'lláh uses this clear allusion to Christ's words to emphasize the contrast between believers and disbelievers, as a judgement of His oppressors, and to say that people should direct their efforts towards those who will be receptive to His Cause.

4 Beware lest the sayings of the heedless sadden thee.
5 Be thou steadfast in the Cause, and teach the people with consummate wisdom.
6 Thus enjoineth thee the Ruler of earth and heaven.
7 He is in truth the Almighty, the Most Generous.

8 Erelong will God exalt thy remembrance and will inscribe with the Pen of Glory that which thou didst utter for the sake of His love.
9 He is in truth the Protector of the doers of good.

COMMENTARY

'Beware lest the sayings of the heedless sadden thee' suggests, in the context of 'be thou steadfast', that Bahá'u'lláh wants the believer to be careful not to let others undermine his or her faith. The believer is one who has been entrusted with the message of God, which is the remedy for the ills afflicting the body of humankind. So the believer has the responsibility of preserving that message and delivering it to the world.

Bahá'u'lláh enjoins one to be steadfast and arise to teach His Faith with wisdom. He writes:

> God hath prescribed unto every one the duty of teaching His Cause. Whoever ariseth to discharge this duty, must needs, ere he proclaimeth His Message, adorn himself with the ornament of an upright and praiseworthy character, so that his words may attract the hearts of such as are receptive to his call. Without it, he can never hope to influence his hearers' (*GWB* 335; see also 314).

And in another passage:

> Say: Teach ye the Cause of God, O people of Bahá, for God hath prescribed unto every one the duty of proclaiming His Message, and regardeth it as the most meritorious of all deeds. Such a deed is acceptable only when he that teacheth the Cause is already a firm believer in God, the Supreme Protector, the Gracious, the Almighty. He hath, moreover, ordained that His Cause be taught through the power of men's utterance, and not through resort to violence (*GWB* 278).

Frequently, when Bahá'u'lláh refers to the teaching of His Faith, emphasis is placed on exercising wisdom (*GWB* 289, 296; *TB* 143).

Bahá'u'lláh has referred to those who have arisen against His Faith, imprisoned Him and even put to death His followers, yet He counsels His followers to teach His Faith with wisdom. They are His hosts, His army, so to speak, but there is no command to resist or take up arms. In fact, violence is forbidden. Their faith is their only shield, their only sword the Word of God.

Bahá'u'lláh states that the command to be steadfast and teach His Cause has been enjoined by God, 'the Ruler of earth and heaven'. The traditional understanding of God as creator suggests that 'earth and heaven' could be interpreted as the physical earth and the universe around the earth. However, this verse can also be interpreted as referring to Bahá'u'lláh, who speaks as God's mediator on earth. From this point of view, the title 'Ruler of earth and heaven', takes on a spiritual significance unrelated to material reality. Bahá'u'lláh states, 'by the term "earth" is meant the earth of understanding and knowledge, and by "heavens" the heavens of divine Revelation' (*KI* 48). Thus 'earth and heaven' concerns the distinction between the world of human understanding and the world of God's Revelation. Bahá'u'lláh is the ruler of spiritual truth, the ruler of the hearts of those who believe in Him and the ruler of the heaven of religion. He rules the devoted teachers of His Faith who are the stars of guidance in the heaven of His religion.

Bahá'u'lláh states He is 'in truth the Almighty, the Most Generous'. This may be a reference to God's might and generosity or to Bahá'u'lláh as one Who manifests God's might and generosity. His might can be seen in the power and invincibility of His Revelation. His Revelation has power to transform people's lives completely and to withstand the opposition of His persecutors. His generosity can be seen in the gift of His Revelation, which

Bahá'ís regard as 'the fountain of the water of life' for the whole world.

With the words, 'Erelong will God exalt thy remembrance and will inscribe with the Pen of Glory that which thou didst utter for the sake of His love', Bahá'u'lláh assures the one who arises to teach His Cause for the love of God that he or she will be remembered and exalted. This verse may refer specifically to the individual in honour of whom this tablet was written. However, it is likely that the promise of spiritual rewards is applicable to anyone who fulfils the spirit of these words.

The title 'Protector of the doers of good', is not intended to mean that calamity will not befall people who do good, for as the Bible reminds us: 'He makes His sun rise on the evil and on the good, and sends rain on the just and on the unjust' (Matt. 5:45). It would be more reasonable to assume that Bahá'u'lláh means He protects the Faithful from the evils of unrighteousness through the guidance of His teachings. He leads us to the path wherein we find righteousness, which is its own reward.

XXIII

1 Give My remembrance to the one named Murád and say: Blessed art thou, O Murád, inasmuch as thou didst cast away the promptings of thine own desire and hast followed Him Who is the Desire of all mankind.

COMMENTARY

This verse appears to be an assurance from Bahá'u'lláh to someone called Murád.[125] Bahá'u'lláh wishes him to know that he is blessed because he has renounced his own desires in order to follow the teachings of Bahá'u'lláh.[126]

The phrase, 'didst cast away the promptings of thine own desire', means a turning away from what is unworthy and a turning towards higher spiritual aspirations. 'Abdu'l-Bahá explains:

---

125. This writer is unaware of any information about or other references pertaining to this person at this time.

126. Stephen Lambden writes: 'In this section of the *Lawh-i-Aqdas* Bahá'u'lláh addresses Murád in a sentence in which a repetitive utilization of the sense of the noun/name Murád is registered in the Arabic. In Arabic the name Murád, signifying "Purposed/ Intended/ Designed/ Willed/ Desired", is formed from the Arabic root RWD/RAD. The same word, *murád*, occurs twice in the address to Murád at the places indicated: "Blessed art thou, O Murád, inasmuch as thou didst cast away the promptings of thine own DESIRE (= Arabic *murád*) and hast followed Him Who is the DESIRE (= Arabic *murád*) of all mankind." The Arabic noun *murád* thus occurs three times in this sentence; once as a proper name (Murád) and twice with the sense of desire/ Desire. The Bahá'í Murád cast aside his own *desire*, his own self or name, and turned to his Divine namesake as the "*Desire* of all mankind" (*murád al-ᶜalamín*), to Bahá'u'lláh.'

COMMENTARY – XXIII

In man there are two natures; his spiritual or higher nature and his material or lower nature. In one he approaches God, in the other he lives for the world alone. Signs of both these natures are to be found in men. In his material aspect he expresses untruth, cruelty and injustice; all these are the outcome of his lower nature. The attributes of his divine nature are shown forth in love, mercy, kindness, truth and justice, one and all being expressions of his higher nature. Every good habit, every noble quality belongs to man's spiritual nature, whereas all his imperfections and sinful actions are born of his material nature. If a man's divine nature dominates his human nature, we have a saint.[127]

In paragraphs XX–XXIII, Bahá'u'lláh directed His message to those who have turned towards and recognized His Faith. He pointed out the attacks of His adversaries to demonstrate the invincibility of God's Faith, perhaps indicating a fulfilment of 'the beast, the kings of the earth, and their armies' having 'gathered together to make war against Him' but being defeated by 'the sword which proceeded' from His 'mouth' (Rev. 19).[128] Now, in the next and last paragraph, Bahá'u'lláh outlines what is, in effect, the condition of the believer who has entered the Kingdom of God.

---

127. *The Reality of Man*, p. 24.
128. It is not the purpose of this commentary to interpret the Book of Revelation. However, it appears reasonable to assert that the opposition to Christ's return, His victory, and the establishment of the millennial kingdom described in chapters 19–22 are, from a Bahá'í point of view, references to Bahá'u'lláh. For example, Bahá'u'lláh refers to Himself as the 'King of Kings' (Shoghi Effendi, PDC pp. 26, 103) and 'Lord of Lords' (Shoghi Effendi, PDC pp. 31, 52), which are the titles mentioned in Rev. 19:16.
Who then is the 'beast'? Shoghi Effendi writes: 'Anyone who violently and determinedly sought to oppose the Manifestation could be called an "anti-Christ" such as the Vazir in the Báb's day, Hájí Mírzá Áqásí ' (LG pp. 367–8). This could probably also be said with reference to the beast mentioned in Revelation 19. 'Abdu'l-Bahá interprets Rev. 11–12 as referring to Islam, the 'great red dragon' being the Umayyad Dynasty which did great harm to Islam (SAQ ch. 13).

AN INTRODUCTION TO PARAGRAPH XXIV

This is the final paragraph of the *Lawḥ-i-Aqdas*. In these concluding verses, Bahá'u'lláh enumerates the spiritual conditions which lead to a state of blessedness. In each verse Bahá'u'lláh begins with the word 'Blessed', a manner of presentation which recalls the 'Beatitudes' of Christ.[129] That Bahá'u'lláh intentionally follows the pattern of the Beatitudes in this paragraph is so likely that it deserves special comment. Specifically, the obvious question is, why would Bahá'u'lláh want to conclude His message to the Christians by speaking in a way which reminds them so vividly of one of Jesus's sermons?

There are a number of possible answers. First, Bahá'u'lláh may be intending to remind Christians of a very important spiritual message at the heart of Jesus's ministry and to show that His words are one in spirit with those of Jesus.

To understand this we should first note some basic points about the Beatitudes of Christ. The Beatitudes are a series of verses beginning with the words: 'Blessed are the poor in spirit, for theirs is the kingdom of heaven. Blessed are those who mourn, for they shall be comforted. Blessed are the meek, for they shall inherit the earth' (Matt. 5:3–5). With these and additional verses, Christ expresses

---

129. 'Beatitudes' comes from the Latin 'beatus', meaning 'blessed'.

spiritual qualities which lead one to a state of blessedness. Blessedness is thus the goal and reward of righteousness; it is a condition of spiritual happiness which does not depend on such temporal conditions as material comforts or wealth.[130] These verses, in effect, show where true happiness is to be found. Christ outlines what many people consider to be the opposite of blessedness, such as the states of poverty and persecution. His teachings are in contrast to the idea that material wealth and a life of comfort are the states or signs of being blessed as well as the paths to happiness.[131] His words also serve as an enduring comfort to those whose positions in the world consist of material deprivation and weakness.

Another important point about the Beatitudes is that they form the first verses of the Sermon on the Mount, which is the longest and fullest continuous presentation of Jesus's teachings in the New Testament (Matt. 5–7).[132] This sermon contains some of the best-known teachings of Jesus. For example, it contains the Lord's Prayer, the golden rule, and the important exhortations on turning the other cheek, going the extra mile and loving one's enemies, among others. Based on these observations about the message of the Beatitudes and the Sermon on

---

130. The word 'blessed' can convey a range of meaning from made holy or sacred to blissful or simply fortunate, happy and comforted. J. C. Lambert expresses a more precise meaning with these words: 'As distinguished from happiness (q.v.), blessedness denotes a state of fruition that is purer and deeper, and free from the accidents of time and circumstances to which happiness is exposed' (*Encyclopedia of Religion and Ethics*, vol. II, p. 675, see Blessedness).

131. 'Abdu'l-Bahá stated: 'The poor are beloved by our heavenly Father. When Christ came upon the earth, those who believed in Him and followed Him were the poor and lowly, showing that the poor were near to God. . . . Their lives are full of difficulties, their trials continual, their hopes are in God alone. Therefore, you must assist the poor as much as possible, even by sacrifice of yourself. No deed of man is greater before God than helping the poor. Spiritual conditions are not dependent upon the possession of worldly treasures or the absence of them. When one is physically destitute, spiritual thoughts are more likely. Poverty is a stimulus toward God' (*PUP* p. 216).

132. It is disputed that Matt. 5–7 is actually a 'sermon'. Ivor Powell, *Matthew's Majestic Gospel*, pp. 89–90.

the Mount, it is probably safe to say that Bahá'u'lláh is calling attention to the fact that, in essence, His spiritual message is one with that of Christ.

A second reason for making a parallel with Jesus's sermon may have been to suggest the establishment of a new covenant, which is an important part of Bahá'u'lláh's Revelation. It has often been observed that the Sermon on the Mount itself parallels in significance the Law, or the teachings of God, coming down from Mount Sinai. For example, the Christian commentator Daniel Patte writes that 'by setting Jesus's teaching "on the mountain" Matthew suggests that Jesus is like Moses on Mt. Sinai'. In this way Matthew presents the Sermon on the Mount as the giving of a new covenant by a new Moses.[133] Thus Bahá'u'lláh's words, expressed in a form similar to the Beatitudes, recall the Sermon on the Mount, and in doing so indicate the establishment of a new covenant.

A third possible reason may have been to convey that at the heart of Bahá'u'lláh's message is the Kingdom of God. Much, if not the entire message, of Jesus's Sermon on the Mount concerns attaining the Kingdom of God (e.g. 5:3, 10, 20 and 7:21). There have been many interpretations of this sermon and its teachings about the Kingdom of God. This commentary is not the place to consider the differing views that have been put forward.[134] What should be said

---

133. Daniel Patte, *The Gospel According to Matthew: A Structural Commentary on Matthew's Faith*, p. 61. Samuel Tobias Lachs writes: 'Matthew's setting for the Sermon on a mountain is intended to parallel the giving of the Law at Mount Sinai', *A Rabbinic Commentary on the New Testament*, p. 67. For how the Beatitudes of Christ parallel Rabbinic teachings, see pp. 68–78.

134. Robert A. Guelich observes: 'Familiarity, however, does not insure understanding. The sea of literature on the Sermon demonstrates that the meaning of the Sermon is anything but self-evident. So vast is this literary sea that no one has undertaken the task of charting the waters by writing a complete history of the Sermon's interpretation' ('Interpreting the Sermon on the Mount', *Interpretation: A Journal of Bible and Theology*, April 1987, vol. XLI, no. 2, p. 117).

is that, from a Bahá'í point of view, Bahá'u'lláh's writings offer insights which clarify much of Jesus's message. Perhaps what will appear most revolutionary to many Christians is that the millennial kingdom, the Kingdom of God on earth that they await, has already been ushered in by Bahá'u'lláh. This claim is very evident in His words, 'O people of the Gospel! They who were not in the Kingdom have now entered it, whilst We behold you, in this day, tarrying at the gate' (Shoghi Effendi, PDC 106).

It has been a long-standing belief among many Christians that, while Jesus brought a spiritual kingdom, when He returns He will establish a visible kingdom with outward splendour and power. While this expectation is essentially sound from a Bahá'í point of view, its establishment in the outward, visible world occurs as the result of its establishment in the hearts of Bahá'u'lláh's followers. Jesus's Kingdom also acquired, in time, visible evidence of its presence, such as the buildings and institutions of the Church, the development of Christian charities and transformations in human relations.

Ultimately, the Kingdom of God is within, and outward appearances in the world around us only result from the inner conversion that takes place first. The Kingdom of God which Christ established in the hearts of His followers is the same in spirit as the Kingdom Bahá'u'lláh has established. Nevertheless, prophecy suggests that the Kingdom will also be established to a greater degree and permanence with Jesus's second coming, that is, with the appearance of Bahá'u'lláh. The prophecies of the Bible indicate that peace will be established throughout the entire world along with a divinely ordained administration of the world's affairs (e.g. Isa. ch. 2; Rev. chs. 20–1). In fact, even today, there are outward signs developing in the Bahá'í world community, such as the growth and development of the divinely ordained Bahá'í Administrative Order, which Bahá'ís regard as no less than the initial steps towards a visible establishment of the Kingdom of God on earth. At the same time, however, such outward signs should not lead us to forget that the Scriptures tell us the Kingdom of God is within us (Luke 17:20–1).[135]

Perhaps by reminding us of the words of Christ, Bahá'u'lláh wishes also to remind us that spiritually, the fundamental nature of the Kingdom of God has not changed.

These observations about the important spiritual message of the Sermon on the Mount, the establishment of a new Covenant, and the Kingdom of God all concern the overall implications of why Bahá'u'lláh may have chosen to parallel Jesus's presentation as it was recorded in Matthew. More specifically, in looking to see how Bahá'u'lláh's words parallel that portion of Jesus's sermon known as the Beatitudes, it can be said that the emphasis in the words of both Christ and Bahá'u'lláh is essentially the same. Both point to important spiritual qualities, a way of righteous living, and the value of persevering through hardships on the religious path. They define the way to discipleship, that is, how a believer should be characterized, the conditions for entrance into the Kingdom of God, and how one should serve God.

---

135. It is not surprising that Bahá'ís standing on Mount Carmel in Israel at the Bahá'í World Centre are compelled by their beliefs to see a literal fulfilment of Isaiah's prophecy: 'Now it shall come to pass in the last days, that the mountain of the LORD's house shall be established in the top of the mountains' (Isa. 2:2, KJV). The Bahá'í pilgrims literally come from 'all nations' and 'flow to it' (Isa. 2:2). And this is literally the seat of the Bahá'í Administrative Order from which 'out of Zion' goes forth 'the law' (Isa. 2:3). But can we not also see a spiritual message in Isaiah's prophecy involving eternal truths which extend beyond any literal interpretations? Did not Jesus send forth a law from the Mount, and did not the nations flow unto it, and was it not established above everything that people regarded as exalted? And in the same way Bahá'u'lláh, and for that matter all the Prophets, have sent forth the Word of God, His laws and teachings for the healing of the nations. Christ said that 'My Kingdom is not of this world' (John 18:36). Surely this does not mean that at His second coming He will appear with a Kingdom that is of this world. The divinely established Kingdom is not a kingdom 'of this world'. Worldly kingdoms, the kingdoms of human making, are 'of this world'. Bahá'u'lláh's Kingdom is a divine Kingdom and, in that way, it is even as Christ's Kingdom.

1 Say: Blessed the slumberer who is awakened by My Breeze.

COMMENTARY

If there is a difference between Bahá'u'lláh's presentation of Beatitudes and that of Christ, it is the clearer emphasis placed on the recognition of His Cause. Only in verse 5:11 of Jesus's Beatitudes does Christ say 'for My sake', whereas Bahá'u'lláh's language continually suggests the need for a strong and specific personal commitment or relationship to His Revelation. Acceptance of Bahá'u'lláh Himself is brought to the core of the spiritual path and identified with the attainment of the blessings of God. This emphasis is seen in the first verse, 'Blessed the slumberer who is awakened by *My Breeze*' (emphasis added). Here the state of slumber is used metaphorically to represent the condition of being spiritually dormant or inactive: the 'slumber of negligence' (*KI* 196). Blessedness is attained by leaving or ending this condition and responding to, being 'awakened' by, Bahá'u'lláh's Revelation. This type of metaphor is frequently used by Bahá'u'lláh. For example He writes: 'O Son of Man! Many a day hath passed over thee whilst thou hast busied thyself with thy fancies and idle imaginings. How long art thou to slumber on thy bed? Lift up thine head from slumber, for the Sun hath risen to the zenith; haply it may shine upon thee with the light of beauty' (*KI* 228, *HWA* No. 62). The words of Bahá'u'lláh seem to be foreseen in this prophecy, 'Arise, shine; for your light has come! And the glory of the LORD is risen upon you' (Isa. 60:1).

2 Blessed the lifeless one who is quickened through My reviving breaths.

COMMENTARY

Here again we find the same type of metaphor, where the condition of being without faith is likened to being lifeless. The state of lifelessness concerns the condition of the individual's spiritual life. These words of Bahá'u'lláh reveal the metaphorical content of His terminology:

> How strange and pitiful! Behold, all the people are imprisoned within the tomb of self, and lie buried beneath the nethermost depths of worldly desire! Wert thou to attain to but a dewdrop of the crystal waters of divine knowledge, thou wouldst readily realize that true life is not the life of the flesh but the life of the spirit. For the life of the flesh is common to both men and animals, whereas the life of the spirit is possessed only by the pure in heart who have quaffed from the ocean of faith and partaken of the fruit of certitude. This life knoweth no death, and this existence is crowned by immortality (KI 120).

The phrase, 'quickened through My reviving breaths', has roots reaching back to the beginnings of Genesis: 'And the Lord God formed man of the dust of the ground, and breathed into his nostrils the breath of life; and man became a living being' (Gen. 2:7). Here and elsewhere breath is the sign of physical life (see Gen. 6:17), but also symbolizes the spirit of God in a person or the divine inspiration of Scripture. Paul says that Scripture is given by the inspiration of God (2 Tim. 3:16). The word 'inspiration', from the Greek 'theopneustos', literally means God-breathed or divinely breathed.[136] The same

---

136. 'Abdu'l-Bahá writes that 'the pure and reviving breath of His [Jesus's] mouth conferred eternal life' (SDC pp. 44–5), and in another passage He refers to the 'sweet and holy breathings of the Spirit of God (Jesus)' (SDC p. 80), 'the

symbolic meaning may be found in passages where Bahá'u'lláh uses the phrases, 'the Breathings of the Divine Spirit' (*GWB* 99) and 'them whom the breath of the verses of God hath quickened' (*GWB* 40). Thus 'Blessed the lifeless one who is quickened through My reviving breaths' means: Blessed is the person who attains the life of faith through the inspiration of Bahá'u'lláh's Revelation.

3 Blessed the eye that is solaced by gazing at My beauty.

COMMENTARY

In this verse Bahá'u'lláh expresses the blessing of those who come to understand and appreciate the beauty of His Revelation. This understanding serves as a solace to the believer, that is it serves to comfort, or to ease and relieve the distresses of life, such as the loneliness and anxiety which people sometimes experience in the quest for meaning.

The word 'eye' is a manner of speaking suggesting one's inner or spiritual perception, such as is expressed in Paul's words, 'the eyes of your understanding being enlightened' (Eph. 1:18). In other passages Bahá'u'lláh refers to the 'eye of the heart' (*KI* 57), the 'eye of justice' (*KI* 58), the 'eye of man's understanding' (*KI* 74) and the 'eye of divine and spiritual discernment' (*KI* 140). The spiritual significance of the words 'eyes' and 'ears' becomes apparent in this explanation of the healing miracles performed by Christ. 'Abdu'l-Bahá writes:

Christ transformed the eye which was blind into a

---

life-giving breaths of the Messiah' (*SDC* p. 45), and 'at the touch of Jesus's breath the unmindful dead that lay in the graves of their ignorance lifted up their heads to receive eternal life' (*SDC* p. 80).

seeing one, rendered the ear which was formerly deaf, attentive, and made the hard, callous heart tender and sensitive. In other words, the meaning is that although the people possess external eyes, yet the insight, or perception, of the soul is blind; although the outer ear hears, the spiritual hearing is deaf; although they possess conscious hearts, they are without illumination; and the bounties of Christ save souls from these conditions (*PUP* 444).

When Bahá'u'lláh refers to His 'beauty', this is not a reference to His physical appearance but, rather, to His divine nature, that aspect of His reality which reveals God. Bahá'u'lláh makes this distinction with these words: 'When I contemplate, O my God, the relationship that bindeth me to Thee, I am moved to proclaim to all created things "verily I am God!"; and when I consider my own self, lo, I find it coarser than clay!' (*WOB* 113). The word 'beauty' appears frequently in Bahá'u'lláh's writings, for example: 'the beauty of Jesus' (*GWB* 20). Bahá'u'lláh's prophetic fulfilment of Scripture, 'the promised Beauty' (*GWB* 17) and in relation to His Revelation, 'God, Who hath formed and fashioned them, and sent down unto them this most effulgent, this most Holy, and manifest Revelation of His beauty' (*GWB* 294).

At its heart, the verse 'Blessed the eye that is solaced by gazing at My beauty', reveals the prophetic fulfilment of Isaiah's words, 'Your eyes will see the King in His beauty' (Isa. 33:17).

4 Blessed the wayfarer who directeth his steps towards the Tabernacle of My glory and majesty.

COMMENTARY

Here Bahá'u'lláh speaks of the blessing of the person who seeks 'the Tabernacle' of His 'glory and majesty'. The 'wayfarer', meaning a person who undertakes a journey, especially on foot, probably represents one who actively goes out in search of the truth and/or journeys from a condition of searching to a place of faith. However, it may be that 'seeks' is not a good equivalent of 'directeth his steps'. The intended meaning may actually involve a more purposeful, more active practice of Bahá'u'lláh's teachings.

The word 'Tabernacle' may have a wide meaning embracing His Cause, His Revelation, and/or Himself.[137] The words, 'the Tabernacle of My glory' call to mind the words of Exodus, 'Then the cloud covered the tabernacle of meeting, and the glory of the LORD filled the tabernacle' (Exod. 40:34). If Bahá'u'lláh is using the Tabernacle as a symbol of His Revelation, which is very probable, then 'the Tabernacle of My glory' suggests that God's glory has once again 'filled' His religion or is manifest in the Revelation of Bahá'u'lláh.

Bahá'u'lláh also uses the Tabernacle as a symbol to signify the place of His presence or His Faith, and in this way it expresses the place of God's presence among us. This type of symbolism, in concept, suggests a parallel to the spiritual significance of the Tabernacle in the Old Testament.[138] This is important because the re-

---

137. See e.g. PM p. 139, KI pp. 103–4, ESW p. 145.
138. This parallel is clearest from an exclusively conceptual interpretation of Bahá'u'lláh's words. A number of different words are translated as 'tabernacle' in the Bahá'í writings, as is also the case in the Bible. In some cases a clear link is implied between the Arabic terminology and context of the Bahá'í writings, and the terminology and symbolism of the Old Testament Tabernacle and the Temple mentioned in prophecy (especially Zech. 6:12) both conceptually and linguistically (see Shoghi Effendi, GPB pp. 110, 213). In other cases,

establishment of the Tabernacle figures prominently in biblical prophecy (Rev. 21:3).[139]

If we are to appreciate its significance it is important to understand its origin and symbolism. After Moses led the Jews out of captivity, God instructed Him to organize the building of an elaborate tent. This tent came to be called the Tabernacle. According to the Bible, when Moses had finished building the Tabernacle as commanded by God, 'Then the cloud covered the tabernacle of meeting, and the glory of the Lord filled the tabernacle' (Exod. 40:34). In this way, the Lord had come to dwell among His people.

In some specific cases in Bahá'u'lláh's writings the symbolism of the Tabernacle or Temple is directly equated with the Law of God (prophesied in Isaiah 2:3) which He has revealed, and the propitiatory aspect of His sacrifice which He has made for humankind.[140] This symbolism appropriately parallels the Old Testament Tabernacle, because that is where the Ark of the Covenant was originally kept (the receptacle containing the tablets of the Law of God which Moses brought down from Mount Sinai). It is also where the High Priest offered sacrifices to God to atone for the sins of the people.[141]

---

as here in verse XXIV:4, the correlation is less certain. In the opinion of this writer the conceptual link is clear, and there is even a similar terminology evident between the original Arabic and Greek, which supports the link, especially to Rev. 21:3. But in other cases, such as in verses XVIII:6 and XXIV:8, the original Arabic is probably no more an allusion to the Tabernacle of Exodus than the Hebrew word translated 'tabernacle' in Isa. 4:6 (KJV).

139. In John's vision he sees the New Jerusalem 'coming down out of heaven' (Rev. 21:1) in which he also sees 'the tabernacle of God' (Rev. 21:1). It should be noted that the Temple is symbolically the equivalent of the Tabernacle. Zechariah (6:12) prophesies the re-establishment of the Temple, but that this does not mean a literal physical structure, as many believe, is indicated by Rev. 21:22. See also Shoghi Effendi, *GPB* pp. 110, 213. 'Abdu'l-Bahá correlates the prophecies of Rev. 21 to the Bahá'í Faith (see *SWA* pp. 12–13).

140. See Shoghi Effendi, *GPB*, p. 213.

141. From the Christian point of view, the offering of sacrifices in the temple rightly ended with the sacrifice of Jesus on the Cross (Heb. ch. 9).

COMMENTARY – XXIV

An immaterial and symbolic concept of the Tabernacle is most likely at the heart of the Exodus description. However, it is a matter of history that the function of the original Tabernacle was established later in the building of the Temple in Jerusalem, which was a material building.[142] In Christianity, Jesus (John 2:19–21) and the Church or the Cause of God among the believers (2 Cor. 6:16) represent the Tabernacle, and its equivalent, the Temple. This transition reveals an evolution from the Judaic physical Tabernacle located in a finite geographical place to the Christian spiritual concept of the Tabernacle – a 'more perfect tabernacle not made with hands, that is, not of this creation' (Heb. 9:11).[143] This spiritual significance is re-established and continues in the Bahá'í Faith.

---

142. The actual Jewish Temple building in Jerusalem was destroyed by the Romans in AD 70 and never rebuilt. Hence some Christians expect Zech. 6:12 to be fulfilled by the literal rebuilding of the Temple in Jerusalem. However, it would seem more in accordance with Scripture that the true Tabernacle was not the physical building in Jerusalem, but rather the Faith of God which had already been destroyed by disobedience to God's teachings. This disobedience manifested itself most in the Jewish opposition to Christ. The Crucifixion was the destruction of the Temple (John 2:19–21), and the establishment of the Church (symbolized by the Resurrection) was in effect Christ's rebuilding of that Temple. Hence the decline of religion in every age is the destruction of the Temple and the appearance of a new Manifestation of God is the rebuilding of the Temple. From this symbolic point of view, the prophecy of Zech. 6:12 has a more universal and eternal meaning not bound to a single outward or historical meaning.

143. 'The religion of Moses seems to be instituted for a particular country as well as for a single nation; and if a strict obedience had been paid to the order that every male, three times in the year, should present himself before the Lord Jehovah, it would have been impossible that the Jews could ever have spread themselves beyond the narrow limits of the promised land. That obstacle was indeed removed by the destruction of the temple of Jerusalem', Gibbon, *The Decline and Fall of Rome*, p. 146. The Temple in Jerusalem was destroyed by the Romans following a Jewish uprising against Roman occupation in AD 70. The Jews were expelled from that region, not returning until the nineteenth century. The Temple has never been reconstructed. However, Bahá'ís believe the Temple has been restored spiritually with the appearance of Bahá'u'lláh.

5 Blessed the distressed one who seeketh refuge beneath the shadow of My canopy.

The 'shadow of My canopy' may be a further extension of the symbolic imagery of the Tabernacle mentioned in the previous verse (XXIV:4). This 'canopy' could be the upper part of the Tabernacle and therefore could be understood in a similar way to the Tabernacle described in the Bible.[144] Otherwise, it may be an allusion to the fulfilment of yet another prophecy (Isa. 4:5–6). This will be discussed in the commentary to verse XXIV:8. Whether it alludes to the canopy of the Tabernacle or the canopy referred to in Isaiah 4:5–6, a protective covering is suggested which symbolizes God's spiritual protection and the salvation ensured to those who abide by the Word of God.

6 Blessed the sore athirst who hasteneth to the soft-flowing waters of My loving-kindness.

COMMENTARY

This verse concerns the person who is seeking and who turns to the Revelation of Bahá'u'lláh, which is a sign and outpouring of His loving-kindness. It echoes Matthew 5:6 and reaffirms the assurance that is stated in the words of the Book of Revelation, 'I am the Alpha and the Omega, the Beginning and the End. I will give of the fountain of the water of life freely to him who thirsts' (Rev. 21:6; see also 22:17). The Christian commentator Matthew Henry writes: 'It would be inconsistent with the goodness of God, and his love to his people, to create in them holy desires, and then deny them their proper satisfaction; and

---

144. The Tabernacle in the Bible was originally a tent which was constructed according to very specific standards (Exod. 35–40).

therefore they may be assured that *he will give them of the fountain of the water of life freely.*'[145]

> 7 Blessed the insatiate soul who casteth away his selfish desires for love of Me and taketh his place at the banquet table which I have sent down from the heaven of divine bounty for My chosen ones.

COMMENTARY

The 'insatiate soul' is the person who is never satisfied, who is constantly seeking to draw nearer to God and acquire divine perfections, consumed with spiritual hunger. That one is blessed who gives up the pursuit of 'selfish desires' to take his or her place in the Cause of God in order to partake of the spiritual bounties God has destined for him or her. The language suggests Jesus's words to his followers: 'And I bestow upon you a kingdom, just as My Father bestowed one upon Me, that you may eat and drink at My table in My kingdom, and sit on thrones judging the twelve tribes of Israel' (Luke 22:29–30; see also 1 Cor. 10:21). In a letter to an individual believer, 'Abdu'l-Bahá writes:

> The gates of the Kingdom are opened wide, and every favoured soul is seated at the banquet table of the Lord, receiving his portion of that heavenly feast. Praised be God, thou too art present at this table, taking thy share of the bountiful food of heaven. Thou art serving the Kingdom, and art well acquainted with the sweet savours of the Abhá[146] Paradise ...

---

145. Matthew Henry, *Matthew Henry's Commentary on the Whole Bible*, p. 1984, his italics.
146. 'Abhá is the Arabic superlative of Bahá (meaning "glory") and means "all glorious".' (From a letter from Stephen Lambden.)

Then strive thou with all thy might to guide the people, and eat thou of the bread that hath come down from heaven. For this is the meaning of Christ's words: 'I am the living bread which came down from heaven ... he that eateth of this bread shall live forever' [John 6:51] (*SWA* 57).

The words of 'Abdu'l-Bahá indicate that to take one's 'place at the banquet table' is to partake of the teachings of Bahá'u'lláh. The metaphor suggests how God has prepared His teachings for the world, and invited humankind to share this spiritual food. The banquet table has been sent down from the heaven of 'divine bounty'. The word 'bounty' means that it is an act of generosity, a gift given freely from the 'divine' world, from God.

The term 'chosen ones' means Bahá'u'lláh's followers. They are chosen in that, as followers of Bahá'u'lláh and participators in the Kingdom, they have been called by God to carry out specific spiritual teachings. Speaking to a group of Bahá'ís, 'Abdu'l-Bahá stated:

Verily, God has chosen you for His love and knowledge; God has chosen you for the worthy service of unifying mankind; God has chosen you for the purpose of investigating reality and promulgating international peace; God has chosen you for the progress and development of humanity, for spreading and proclaiming true education, for the expression of love toward your fellow creatures and the removal of prejudice; God has chosen you to blend together human hearts and give light to the human world. The doors of His generosity are wide, wide open to us; but we must be attentive, alert and mindful, occupied with service to all mankind, appreciating the bestowals of God and ever conforming to His will (*PUP* 334–5).

In the Old Testament, the Jews were chosen by God to be the preservers of God's Word and the channel through which people were guided to God. With the coming of Christ, these duties passed to the 'Gentiles', or non-Jewish people, because the mass of the Jews rejected Christ. Isaiah had prophesied that, 'I will also give You as a light to the Gentiles, that You should be My salvation to the ends of the earth' (Isa. 49:6). Since the time of Christ, no single nation has alone been chosen by God to spread the Word.

'Chosen' does not mean those who chose to believe in God, but rather those whom God chose. Christ stated, 'You did not choose Me, but I chose you and appointed you that you should go and bear fruit, and that your fruit should remain, that whatever you ask the Father in My name He may give you' (John 15:16).

In an explanation of the verse, 'For many are called, but few are chosen' (Matt. 20:16), 'Abdu'l-Bahá stated:

> It is from the bounty of God that man[147] is selected for the highest degree; and the differences which exist between men in regard to spiritual progress and heavenly perfections, is also due to the choice of the Compassionate One. For faith, which is life eternal, is a sign of bounty, and not the result of justice. The flame of the fire of love, in this world of earth and water, comes through the power of attraction and not by effort and striving. Nevertheless, by effort and perseverance, knowledge, science, and other perfections can be acquired; but only the light of the Divine Beauty can transport and move the spirits through the force of attraction. Therefore it is said: 'Many are called but few are chosen' (*SAQ*, ch. 32).

'Abdu'l-Bahá continues to explain that the differences between people are not cause for criticism. Even as the differences between plants and animals are acceptable, so

---

147. This concerns both men and women being selected to the highest degree as compared to the mineral, plant, and animal levels of existence.

too, the differences between people are ordained by and acceptable before God.

> The differences among mankind are of two sorts: one is a difference of station, and this difference is not blameworthy. The other is a difference of faith and assurance; the loss of these is blameworthy; for then the soul is overwhelmed by his desires and passions, which deprive him of these blessings and prevent him from feeling the power of attraction of the love of God. Though that man is praiseworthy and acceptable in his station, yet as he is deprived of the perfections of that degree, he will become a source of imperfections, for which he is held responsible (*SAQ*, ch. 32; see also *SWA* 9).

8 Blessed the abased one who layeth fast hold on the cord of My glory; and the needy one who entereth beneath the shadow of the Tabernacle of My wealth.

COMMENTARY

In this verse Bahá'u'lláh speaks of 'the cord of My glory' and 'the Tabernacle of My wealth'. This 'cord' is a metaphor for the spiritual force which acts as a tie or bond between humankind and God. Shoghi Effendi states, 'The word "cord", so often mentioned in the teachings, means both the Faith itself and also the power of the Faith which sustains those who cling to it.'[148] Obedience to the Covenant of God established by Bahá'u'lláh is likely to be at the heart of that force.

The significance of 'glory' in the phrase the 'cord of My glory', can be seen in these words of Bahá'u'lláh: 'The

---

148. From a letter written on behalf of Shoghi Effendi. See *LG*, p. 360.

source of all glory is acceptance of whatsoever the Lord hath bestowed, and contentment with that which God hath ordained' (TB 155). The wealth He speaks of in the phrase 'the Tabernacle of My wealth' is not material wealth but, rather, divine love, the love of God and God's love for us. Bahá'u'lláh writes, 'The essence of wealth is love for Me; whoso loveth Me is the possessor of all things, and he that loveth Me not is indeed of the poor and needy. This is that which the Finger of Glory and Splendour hath revealed' (TB 156).

Bahá'u'lláh holds up Jesus as an example of real wealth, even though, as we know, Jesus had no possessions. In fact, according to the Gospel, Jesus was poor and had not even a place to sleep, 'the Son of Man has nowhere to lay His head' (Matt. 8:20). Yet, referring to His poverty, Bahá'u'lláh says: 'By the righteousness of Thousands of treasures circle round this poverty, and a myriad kingdoms of glory yearn for such abasement!' He goes on to say that if one were to appreciate the significance of Christ's material poverty and His spiritual wealth one would 'surely forsake the world and all that is therein and, as the Phoenix, wouldst consume thyself in the flames of that undying Fire' (KI 130–1). In other words, the worst poverty is not material poverty but the poverty of being without God. Christ was poor in material things but rich in the love of God. Moreover, His poverty, like the suffering all the Prophets endure for our sakes, testifies to the abundant wealth of God's love for us.

From this understanding of wealth, one can see that a poor person may be rich and a rich person may be poor. Bahá'u'lláh explains, 'By "riches" therefore is meant independence of all else but God, and by "poverty" the lack of things that are of God' (KI 132). Thus, the 'Tabernacle of My wealth' is a spiritual wealth consisting of an abundant devotion and love of God.[149]

---

149. The understanding that true wealth is in proportion to one's love and devotion to God is evident in many passages of the Bible. Particularly clear statements on this theme are expressed in words attributed to Jesus in the Book of Revelation. See Rev. 2:9 and 3:17.

The words 'My wealth' may mean the love of God which we learn from the Prophets, as just explained, but it may also mean God's love for us. This is suggested by the phrase itself, which may be an allusion to prophecy. Bahá'u'lláh speaks of the one who 'entereth beneath the shadow of the Tabernacle' of His wealth. These words evoke Isaiah's prophetic words, 'For over all the glory there will be a covering. And there will be a tabernacle[150] for shade in the daytime from the heat, for a place of refuge, and for a shelter from storm and rain' (Isa. 4:5–6). Bahá'u'lláh's Revelation fulfils this prophecy in that it is a spiritual canopy under which the seeker can find refuge from the suffering that is caused by the uncertainties of life.

9 **Blessed the ignorant one who seeketh the fountain of My knowledge; and the heedless one who cleaveth to the cord of My remembrance.**

COMMENTARY

In this verse the fountain symbolizes Bahá'u'lláh's Revelation and/or Himself as a Manifestation of God, and His knowledge concerns the knowledge of God: 'The source of all learning is the knowledge of God, exalted be His Glory, and this cannot be attained save through the knowledge of His Divine Manifestations' (*TB* 156).

As for the cord of His Remembrance, Bahá'u'lláh speaks of true remembrance with these words, 'True remembrance is to make mention of the Lord, the All-

---

[150]. The Hebrew word here, translated 'tabernacle', like the Arabic word translated tabernacle in the *Lawḥ-i-Aqdas* (i.e. in this specific case XXIV:8 and also XVIII:6), does not appear to mean specifically the Tabernacle of Exodus, but rather a large tent or covering. It simply symbolizes divine shelter by using the image of a large protective covering which, like the covering of a tent, provides shelter from scorching heat or storms.

Praised, and forget aught else beside Him' (TB 155). Thus the blessing is upon those who seek the knowledge of God from His Manifestation, Bahá'u'lláh, and overcome their neglect of spiritual matters in remembering God and obeying His teachings.

10 Blessed the soul that hath been raised to life through My quickening breath and hath gained admittance into My heavenly Kingdom.

COMMENTARY

This verse expresses the assurance of blessedness to those who attain the life of faith through Bahá'u'lláh's 'quickening breaths', that is, the inspiration of His Revelation which gives and restores life. With the words, 'hath gained admittance into My heavenly Kingdom', Bahá'u'lláh speaks of the spiritual condition of the believer. He is the King, and the hearts of His servants are His Kingdom.

'Abdu'l-Bahá writes that because of the appearance of Bahá'u'lláh, 'the splendours of the Kingdom were shed over east and west'. He continues: 'Those who had eyes to see rejoiced at the glad tidings and cried out: "O blessed, blessed are we!", and they witnessed the inner reality of all things, and uncovered the mysteries of the Kingdom' (SWA 33). Concerning the difference between the Kingdom of God and this world, 'Abdu'l-Bahá writes:

> O thou who seeketh the Kingdom of heaven! This world is even as the body of man, and the Kingdom of God is as the spirit of life. See how dark and narrow is the physical world of man's body, and what a prey it is to diseases and ills. On the other hand, how fresh and bright is the realm of the human spirit. Judge thou from this metaphor how the world

of the Kingdom hath shone down, and how its laws have been made to work in this nether realm. Although the spirit is hidden from view, still its commandments shine out like rays of light upon the world of the human body. In the same way, although the Kingdom of heaven is hidden from the sight of this unwitting people, still, to him who seeth with the inner eye, it is plain as day (*SWA* 192).

And in another passage, 'Abdu'l-Bahá writes with regard to those who believe in Bahá'u'lláh: 'O ye peoples of the Kingdom! How many a soul expended all its span of life in worship, endured the mortification of the flesh, longed to gain an entry into the Kingdom, and yet failed, while ye, with neither toil nor pain nor self-denial, have won the prize and entered it.' Referring to the time of Christ He adds, 'It is even as in the time of the Messiah, when the Pharisees and the pious were left without a portion, while Peter, John, and Andrew, given neither to pious worship nor ascetic practice, won the day. Wherefore, thank ye God for setting upon your heads the crown of glory everlasting, for granting unto you this immeasurable grace' (*SWA* 18–19).

11 Blessed the man whom the sweet savours of reunion with Me have stirred and caused to draw nigh unto the Dayspring of My Revelation.

COMMENTARY

That person is blessed who sees the revelation of God's love, power and glory in the sacrifices of Bahá'u'lláh's life, such as His imprisonments and exiles, and consequently is 'caused to draw nigh unto the Dayspring' of His Revelation.

The 'sweet savours of reunion' may mean sweet savours,

as in the sacrificial offering made to God for the redemption of humankind. The biblical roots of the phrase 'sweet savours' were discussed in the commentary on verse XIX:6. The implication is that the sacrifice of Bahá'u'lláh is the channel through which humankind is being reconciled and reunited with God.

12 Blessed the ear that hath heard and the tongue that hath borne witness and the eye that hath seen and recognized the Lord Himself, in His great glory and majesty, invested with grandeur and dominion.

COMMENTARY

This verse refers to the person who has heard (or understood) and testified ('borne witness') to his belief; and the person who has seen, or perceived, and recognized the spiritual sovereignty of Bahá'u'lláh, 'the Lord Himself, in His great spiritual glory and majesty, invested with grandeur and dominion'. Bahá'u'lláh's 'grandeur' refers to His intrinsic nobility of character, and His 'dominion' is the hearts of those He has changed.

Many Christians who expect Christ to return *visibly* in the sky with power and great glory, find it difficult to see that Bahá'u'lláh is the fulfilment of biblical prophecy. This may be why Bahá'u'lláh refers especially to the blessedness of the one whose 'eye' hath 'seen and recognized the Lord Himself, in His great glory and majesty, invested with grandeur and dominion'. According to the Bible, when Christ returns, 'all the tribes of the earth' will 'see' Him (Matt. 24:30); that 'He is coming with clouds, and every eye will see Him, and they also who pierced Him'(Rev. 1:7). In the commentary on verse XXIV:3 it has been observed that the 'eye' that 'sees' Him is the inner eye, so to speak, the 'eyes of your understanding' (Eph.

1:18). From this perspective, everyone who investigates the Bahá'í Faith and understands Bahá'u'lláh's spiritual reality will perceive His truth. However, the prophecy, and especially Revelation 1:7, appears to be speaking of an appearance that is visible to all people. The prophecy even states that 'they also who pierced Him' will see His appearance.

Perhaps what should be kept in mind is that the prophecies of the Bible state that when Christ returns there will be those who will oppose Him (Rev. 19). This indicates that not everyone will believe in Him even when He returns. From this simple deduction, it is difficult to imagine that Christ could literally return in the sky, in such an extraordinary manner, and yet some will still remain who oppose Him and disbelieve.[151] Why would everyone not yield to such clear and forceful evidence? What seems more probable is that these prophecies indicate that Christ's appearance will be openly proclaimed to all people. It will not remain a secret preserved for only a special few. Bahá'u'lláh openly proclaimed His Cause, and His followers have continued to spread His message to all the world. No one needs to seek Him 'in the desert' or in hidden 'inner rooms' (Matt. 24:26–7). This is not an esoteric religion, but a Faith for all people.

But how does this explanation account for the prophecy's inclusion of 'they also who pierced Him?' While Christ was on the Cross His side was pierced by the spear of a Roman guard (John 19:34). It is a common Christian interpretation that 'they also who pierced Him' refers to this guard mentioned in John and, according to the Christian commentator Matthew Henry, 'all who have wounded and crucified him afresh by their apostasy from him'.[152] From a Bahá'í point of view, what this verse may

---

151. Bahá'u'lláh explains Matt. 24:30 in the *Kitáb-i-Íqán*, pp. 24–79. He rejects the literal interpretations of these prophecies, pointing out that such literal occurrences would interfere with humankind's free will, pp. 80–1.
152. *Matthew Henry's Commentary on the Whole Bible*, p. 1970.

suggest is that when Christ returns in the world, the spirit of those who opposed Him will also have returned in the world. Such persons will see and hear of His Cause, and like those who heard of Christ in His Day, they will act with contempt. Surely it is indisputable that those who persecuted Bahá'u'lláh are comparable to Jesus's tormentors.

The 'eye that hath seen and recognized the Lord Himself' is the eye that has not been hindered by literal interpretations of prophecy. Bahá'u'lláh states that Scripture is written in symbolic language for a reason:

> Know verily that the purpose underlying all these symbolic terms and abstruse allusions, which emanate from the Revealers of God's holy Cause, hath been to test and prove the peoples of the world; that thereby the earth of the pure and illuminated hearts may be known from the perishable and barren soil. From time immemorial such hath been the way of God amidst His creatures, and to this testify the records of the sacred books (KI 49).

There are several points which support the concept that God uses Scripture to test His servants. Most apparent is the difficulty of interpreting prophecy. Why is prophecy not so clear as to allow only one interpretation? Why does the book of Isaiah, for example, not specify which prophecies refer to Christ's first coming and which to His second coming? Why did none of the Bible's authors say whether prophecy should be interpreted symbolically, or literally? Obviously, either method is possible depending on what we are willing to accept about the world around us. But according to Bahá'u'lláh, the real test of our interpretation of Scripture is whether or not it conforms to the reality of God's plan. The person who rejects the Messiah, because the Messiah's appearance does not conform to his or her interpretation, whether it is based on a literal or a symbolic approach, has been tested and has failed. The soul who is humble enough to reconsider his or her interpretations, and accepts the signs of his or her Lord's divinity, is the one who has been tested and found to be among those whose hearts are 'pure and illuminated'. That person is 'blessed'.

13 Blessed are they that have attained His presence.

COMMENTARY

The word 'presence' appears six times in this translation of the *Lawḥ-i-Aqdas*. Here, in verse XXIV:13, it suggests the religious concept conveyed by the word 'presence' found in other verses, but the word itself is not actually in the original Arabic.[153] Nevertheless, the translation accurately reflects the object of attainment with the words 'His presence'. This is supported in verse XV:9 which states: 'We have summoned all created things to attain the presence of the Lord'. In this earlier verse the word 'presence' is directly stated in the original Arabic.

In verse XV:9, and as suggested in XXIV:13, 'presence' has special significance from the point of view of the New Testament prophecies.[154] The second coming of Christ is often referred to as the 'Parousia'. This term is derived from the Gospel according to Matthew which records that

---

153. The earlier 1913 translation reads, 'Blessed are those who have attained'.

154. With regard to this interpretation, Stephen Lambden expressed the following view: 'In the *Kitáb-i-Íqán* the term "Presence of God" translates the Arabic genitive phrase "liqá'ulláh". It is the important word "liqá'" which is translated "Presence" (as it is twice in the *Lawḥ-i-Aqdas* 1987 ed.; see p. 3). Arabic "liqá'" is the key Arabic technical term indicative of the eschatological meeting/encounter/presence/advent of Divinity. It occurs some 24 times in the Qur'án in connection with the advent of the eschatological "hour" or onset of the Day of Resurrection when God Himself appears on earth, as explained and interpreted in the *Kitáb-i-Íqán*. The term "liqá'" is directly rooted in the Qur'án but does in the Bahá'í view relate to the parousia connected with the second advent of Christ.'

the Apostles ask Christ, 'what will be the sign of Your coming, and the end of the age?' (Matt. 24:3). The word translated as 'coming' from the early Greek manuscripts is 'parousia', which actually means 'presence'.[155] This suggests the close relationship between recognizing Christ's return and attaining His presence. Bahá'u'lláh writes: 'Whoso hath recognized the Day Spring of Divine guidance and entered His holy court hath drawn nigh unto God and attained His Presence, a Presence which is the real Paradise, and of which the loftiest mansions of heaven are but a symbol' (GWB 70). This indicates that 'Blessed are they that have attained His presence' signifies those who have recognized Bahá'u'lláh as the appearance of Christ foretold in Matthew (ch. 24). In response to the Apostles' questions about His coming and the end of the age, Christ also speaks of the coming of the Kingdom of God (see Matt. ch. 25).[156]

The appearance of Christ and the appearance, or establishment, of the Kingdom of God are strongly related to each other in the Bible. This is why attaining this 'presence' involves both recognition of Bahá'u'lláh and entering the Kingdom of God. Earlier in this tablet, Bahá'u'lláh speaks of attaining the 'presence of thy Lord' in connection with 'the Day of Reckoning' (XV:9–10). This suggests that 'His presence' and Christ's return are connected in meaning.

The significance of the words 'His presence' is explained in the *Kitáb-i-Íqán*. Bahá'u'lláh writes: 'By attaining ... to the presence of these holy Luminaries, the "Presence of God" Himself is attained. From their knowledge, the knowledge of God is revealed, and from the light of their countenance, the splendor of the Face of God

---

155. Early translations into Latin used the word 'adventus' which is the root of the word 'advent'. For a discussion of how some Christians have debated this term in recent times, see Carl Olof Jonsson and Wolfgang Herbst, *The Sign of the Last Days – When*.

156. The New Testament sometimes uses the 'kingdom of heaven' which is an alternative with the same meaning (Alan Richardson, ed., *A Theological Word Book of the Bible*, pp. 119–20).

is made manifest' (*KI* 142). Moreover, He writes, 'For the highest and most excelling grace bestowed upon men is the grace of "attaining unto the presence of God" and of His recognition, which has been promised unto all people' (*KI* 138).

14 Blessed the man who hath sought enlightenment from the Day-Star of My Word.

15 Blessed he who hath attired his head with the diadem of My love.

COMMENTARY

That person is blessed who takes Bahá'u'lláh's writings as his or her spiritual guide and who has found and/or characterized his or her life by the love of God.

The 'Day-Star of My Word' means, figuratively, the guidance of His Revelation, which is like the star of the day, that is, the sun. A 'diadem' is a type of headband comparable to a crown, in as much as it is a royal emblem signifying sovereignty.[157] The diadem, or crown, of Bahá'u'lláh's love is a symbol the significance of which is also expressed in the Bible. James writes, 'Blessed is the man who endures temptation; for when he has been proved, he will receive the crown of life which the Lord has promised to those who love Him' (Jas. 1:12). The second coming is the 'crown of rejoicing' (1 Thess. 2:19), and there is the Messianic promise of Peter, 'when the Chief Shepherd appears, you will receive the crown of glory that does not fade away' (1 Pet. 5:4). Isaiah prophesies, 'In that day the LORD of Hosts will be for a crown of glory and a diadem of beauty to the remnant of His people' (Isa. 28:5). Thus Bahá'u'lláh offers the promised

---

157. *Encyclopedia of Religion and Ethics*, G. F. Hill, vol. IV, see Crown, pp. 336–7.

crown, the crown of the love of God. He writes, 'The essence of love is for man to turn his heart to the Beloved One, and sever himself from all else but Him, and desire naught save that which is the desire of his Lord' (TB 155).

16 Blessed is he who hath heard of My grief and hath arisen to aid Me among My people.

COMMENTARY

Bahá'u'lláh states here that the person who aids His Cause is blessed. By 'hath heard of My grief' He may mean those who have heard of His suffering, have believed in Him, and have therefore arisen to assist His Cause. It may also mean, more generally, to have heard of the suffering of any of the believers in Bahá'u'lláh's Cause. Another possible meaning is that 'My grief' may be an allusion to the sorrow caused by those who profess to be believers but act against His teachings. Bahá'u'lláh says that, 'The imprisonment inflicted on this wronged One . . . did to Him no harm nor can it ever do so; nor can the loss of all His earthly goods, His exile, or even His martyrdom and outward humiliation, do Him any hurt. That which can hurt Him are the evil deeds which the beloved of God commit, and which they impute to Him Who is the Sovereign Truth' (GWB 244).

To aid His Cause refers only to such means as are consistent with His teachings. Bahá'u'lláh teaches that violence is not to be used to spread His Cause (GWB 303). He says that His followers should: 'Aid ye your Lord with the sword of wisdom and of utterance. This indeed well becometh the station of man. To depart from it would be unworthy of God, the Sovereign Lord of all, the Glorified' (GWB 296).[158]

158. For further information about non-violence and religion, see J. E. Esslemont, *Bahá'u'lláh and the New Era*, pp. 170–1.

The phrase 'Me among My people' probably does not mean the actual person of Bahá'u'lláh but, rather, His Spirit or Cause among the believers. This is similar to Jesus's words to Paul in his vision on the road to Damascus, which occurs before Paul's conversion. Jesus asks Paul: 'why are you persecuting Me?' (Acts 9:4), when in reality it was not Jesus whom Paul was after but the 'disciples of the Lord' (Acts 9:1). The words of Christ are understandable because the believers are the body of Christ (1 Cor. 12:12–13, 27). Hence, to persecute the believers is to persecute Christ. This could be the same meaning Bahá'u'lláh intends with the words, 'Me among My people'.

17 Blessed is he who hath laid down his life in My path and hath borne manifold hardships for the sake of My Name.

COMMENTARY

To lay down one's life does not necessarily mean to submit to physical death. It could also mean simply to dedicate one's life to the Cause of God, to exercise a high degree of self-renunciation. To bear 'manifold hardships' for the sake of Bahá'u'lláh could also have a wider meaning than just hardships in the context of persecution. For example, it could include hardships involved in the acceptance of extreme difficulties to teach His Faith, such as giving up a profitable job and moving to a remote and unfamiliar part of the world. However, it may be that the traditional view of persecution and martyrdom is primarily intended. This verse bears a strong similarity to Jesus's words, 'Blessed are those who are persecuted for righteousness' sake, for theirs is the kingdom of heaven. Blessed are you when they revile and persecute you, and say all kinds of evil against you falsely for My sake' (Matt. 5:10–11).

The subject of martyrdom appears frequently in the Bahá'í writings. Bahá'u'lláh writes, 'For everything there is a sign. The sign of love is fortitude under My decree and patience under My trials' (*HWA* No.48). And, in another passage He writes, 'Seek a martyr's death in My path, content with My pleasure and thankful for that which I ordain, that thou mayest repose with Me beneath the canopy of majesty behind the tabernacle of glory' (*HWA* No.45). The Bahá'í Faith, like Christianity, has suffered recurring persecutions, and many individuals have sacrificed their lives for their beliefs.[159]

18 Blessed the man who, assured of My Word, hath arisen from among the dead to celebrate My praise.

COMMENTARY

Those who have attained certitude in the Cause of God, who have arisen to a spiritual life, and who celebrate His praise are blessed. Those who have 'arisen from among the dead' are the 'dead in trespasses' (Eph. 2:5; see also 1 Thess. 4:14–17). The meaning of 'arisen from among the dead' is expressed in this explanation by 'Abdu'l-Bahá:

> The world of humanity cannot advance through mere physical powers and intellectual attainments; nay, rather, the Holy Spirit is essential. The divine Father must assist the human world to attain maturity. The body of man is in need of physical and mental energy, but his spirit requires the life and fortifica-

---

[159]. Up to this time such severe persecution has been mostly confined to the Middle East and, primarily, Iran.

tion of the Holy Spirit. Without its protection and quickening the human world would be extinguished. Jesus Christ declared, 'Let the dead bury their dead.' He also said, 'That which is born of the flesh is flesh; and that which is born of the Spirit is spirit.' It is evident, therefore, according to Christ that the human spirit which is not fortified by the presence of the Holy Spirit is dead and in need of resurrection by that divine power; otherwise, though materially advanced to high degrees, man cannot attain full and complete progress (*PUP* 182).

The words, 'hath arisen from among the dead to celebrate My praise', recall the spirit of these words of the king of Judah, Hezekiah, recorded in the book of Isaiah, 'the grave cannot praise thee, death cannot celebrate thee: they that go down into the pit[160] cannot hope for thy truth. The living, the living, he shall praise thee, as I do this day: the father to the children shall make known thy truth' (Isa. 38:18–19, KJV).

19 Blessed is he that hath been enraptured by My wondrous melodies and hath rent the veils asunder through the potency of My might.

COMMENTARY

In this verse, the Revelation of God and His Cause is figuratively likened to music or song. Bahá'u'lláh's 'wondrous melodies' are those spiritual melodies of the Scriptures that people hear in their hearts ('making melody in your heart' Eph. 5:19). Bahá'u'lláh uses the word

---

160. For some Christians this 'pit' is a reference to Hell, what some consider to be a condition and others think to be an actual place. The Bahá'í concept is that Hell is a state of remoteness from God. Bahá'u'lláh writes: 'They say: "Where is Paradise, and where is Hell?" Say: "The one is reunion with Me; the other thine own self"' (*ESW* p. 132).

'melodies' in connection with Scripture when He writes, 'Hearken unto the melodies of the Gospel with the ear of fairness' (*ESW* 143). In another instance, 'Abdu'l-Bahá said to a group of people gathered at a meeting:

> This is a blessed meeting, for these revered souls have come together in complete unity and with an intelligent purpose. It is an occasion of great joy to me. Before me are faces radiant with the glad tidings of God, hearts aglow with the fire of the love of God, ears attuned to the *melodies of the kingdom* [emphasis added] and eyes illumined by the signs and evidences of Divinity (*PUP* 437–8).

People have often referred to music as a universal language. To liken spirituality to melodious music, therefore, is an appropriate analogy. It is universal, bringing happiness to all people.

The person who 'hath rent the veils asunder through the potency' of His might, has overcome the obstacles standing between him and her and the knowledge of God. By 'the potency of [His] might' Bahá'u'lláh means that such a person has overcome obstacles through the influence and understanding of His words and the sacrifice of His life.

20 Blessed is he who hath remained faithful to My Covenant, and whom the things of the world have not kept back from attaining My Court of holiness.

COMMENTARY

Here the state of blessedness is achieved by the person who is faithful to Bahá'u'lláh's Covenant. A covenant is a bond or agreement made between two or more parties. In the religious sense the covenant concerns the relationship between God and humankind. This covenant, or agreement, involves certain promises from God and certain obligations on the part of humankind. Generally, these promises and obligations consist of the spiritual guidance and protection God provides and, in return, faith in and obedience to His teachings.

The Bible records that God established a covenant with the Israelites at Sinai, with Moses as mediator. The details and stipulations of the covenant are described in Exodus, chapters 21–3, and the actual rite is described in chapter 24.

In the rite affirming this covenant, an animal was sacrificed. This animal sacrifice was repeated annually by the high priest of the Jewish Faith to atone for the people's sins. Individual believers also brought offerings to sacrifice to God. However, the sacrifices offered by individual believers were made in the court surrounding or in front of the tabernacle. As noted earlier, only the high priest was allowed to offer sacrifices inside the tabernacle. Thus, it is possible that the 'court of holiness' is also an allusion to the symbolic significance of the biblical tabernacle.

The design of the tabernacle served to show that God was separated from the people by His holiness and that He could only be approached in the ways that He prescribed. The person 'whom the things of the world have not kept back from attaining My court of holiness', is, then, the person who follows Bahá'u'lláh's teachings.

In Christianity Jesus established a new covenant and replaced the repeated animal sacrifices with the sacrifice of His own life on the Cross. Jesus said, 'This is My blood of the new covenant, which is shed for many' (Mark 14:24; see also Heb. 9:22–8).

Bahá'u'lláh is also a mediator of a new covenant, and His sufferings are also a sacrifice made for the establishment of this new covenant.[161] In the Bahá'í Faith the

---

161. See V:2, 3.

COMMENTARY – XXIV

central idea of the Covenant involves the unity of the Faith. By obedience to the Covenant, the Bahá'í Faith will remain one Faith and not be divided into hundreds of conflicting groups, as past religions have been. In the Bahá'í Faith, to create schism is to break the Covenant.

Obedience to the Covenant involves acknowledging and faithfully adhering to the authority of the appointed successor of Bahá'u'lláh. In His Will and Testament Bahá'u'lláh appointed His son, 'Abdu'l-Bahá, as His successor and as the Centre of His Covenant. Bahá'u'lláh established this Covenant so that there would be no divisions in the Bahá'í Faith, and directed His followers to 'refer ye whatsoever ye understand not in the Book to Him Who hath branched from this mighty Stock' (WOB 134). 'Abdu'l-Bahá, in His Will and Testament, appointed His grandson, Shoghi Effendi, to be Guardian of the Bahá'í Faith, 'he is the sign of God, the chosen branch, the guardian of the Cause of God, he unto whom all the Aghṣán,[162] the Afnán,[163] the Hands of the Cause of God[164] and His loved ones must turn.'[165] Although Shoghi Effendi appointed no successor, the Covenant of Bahá'u'lláh is continued in the Administrative Order of the Bahá'í Faith.

Shoghi Effendi points out that:

This Administrative Order is fundamentally different from anything that any Prophet has previously established, inasmuch as Bahá'u'lláh has Himself revealed its principles, established its institutions, appointed the person to interpret His Word and conferred the necessary authority on the body

162. Aghṣán (lit. branches), meaning the descendants of Bahá'u'lláh.
163. Afnán (lit. twigs), a designation signifying the 'members of the family of the Báb descended from his three maternal uncles or the two brothers and sister of his wife' (From the glossary of Momen's The Bábí and Bahá'í Religions, 1844–1944: Some Contemporary Western Accounts, p. 530).
164. 'The Hands of the Cause of God' was a title bestowed on certain individuals for their meritorious service to the Faith (Shoghi Effendi, WOB pp. 110, 147).
165. 'Abdu'l-Bahá, Will and Testament of 'Abdu'l-Bahá, p. 11.

designed to supplement and apply His legislative ordinances. Therein lies the secret of its strength, its fundamental distinction, and the guarantee against disintegration and schism. Nowhere in the sacred scriptures of any of the world's religious systems, nor even in the writings of the Inaugurator of the Bábí Dispensation, do we find any provisions establishing a covenant or providing for an administrative order that can compare in scope and authority with those that lie at the very basis of the Bahá'í Dispensation (WOB 145).[166]

Bahá'u'lláh writes: 'So firm and mighty is this Covenant that from the beginning of time until the present day no religious Dispensation hath produced its like' (WOB 146).

---

166. The supreme governing body of the Bahá'í Administrative Order, the Universal House of Justice, was first elected in 1963. This body is elected democratically by the 'representatives of the faithful' (Shoghi Effendi, WOB p. 154) and is responsible for 'legislating on matters not expressly revealed in the Bahá'í writings' (Ibid., p. 153).

21 Blessed is the man who hath detached himself from all else but Me, hath soared in the atmosphere of My love,[167] hath gained admittance into My Kingdom,[168] gazed upon My realms of glory,[169] quaffed the living waters of My bounty,[170] hath drunk his fill from the heavenly river of My loving providence,[171] acquainted himself with My Cause, apprehended that which I concealed within the treasury of My Words, and hath shone forth from the horizon of divine knowledge engaged in My praise and glorification.[172]

COMMENTARY

This passage is, in some measure, a summary and reiteration of the preceding verses. In the Beatitudes of the Gospel of Matthew, Christ ends the first verse with: 'For theirs is the kingdom of heaven' (Matt. 5:3). In verse 5:10 He repeats this ending. In the same way, Bahá'u'lláh repeats Himself to emphasize His message and make clear His intention. Bahá'u'lláh also refers twice to the Kingdom of God in His beatitudes (XXIV:10, 21).

Bahá'u'lláh stresses renunciation of those things which are contrary to His teachings, devotion to His Cause, attainment to the spiritual or religious life of the Bahá'í Faith (My Kingdom), perception of (gazed upon) the spiritual reality of His station and teachings (My realms of glory), turning (quaffed) to His writings (living waters) for guidance, internalizing (hath drunk his fill) His teachings (heavenly river) according to his or her capacity,

---

167. Cf. 1 Thess. 4:16–17.
168. Cf. Luke 13:24–30.
169. Ch. 21 of the Book of Revelation can be interpreted as a symbolic description of His 'realms of glory'.
170. Cf. Rev. 22:17.
171. Cf. Rev. 22:1.
172. Cf. Isa. 24:15.

acquainting him or herself with His Cause, apprehending the meanings concealed within His words and acquiring the knowledge of God and those things that are spiritual (the horizon of divine knowledge), and engaging in praise and glorification of His Revelation.

22 Verily, he is of Me.
23 Upon him rest My mercy, My loving-kindness, My bounty and My glory.

COMMENTARY

Bahá'u'lláh outlined certain characteristics of a spiritual life and summarized them in verse 21. He now states that these are signs that whoever follows these teachings is of Him, i.e. that such a person is a 'Bahá'í'. However, this does not necessarily mean that to fall short of all these qualities makes one an unacceptable Bahá'í. These characteristics describe the ideal or archetypical Bahá'í: a statement of what is, rather than a statement of what is not. But these ideals are the qualities which constitute true entrance into the kingdom of God. One's blessedness and happiness rest with these ideals. The greater the attainment, the greater the blessedness. It seems reasonable, from this point of view, that a person who is not happy should consider: Am I really in the Kingdom? Happiness may be a good way of determining one's spiritual condition and unhappiness may be a sign that one is drifting from the spiritual path and living too much for the material world.

No person is always happy, and 'Abdu'l-Bahá explains that suffering can actually be beneficial: 'While a man is happy he may forget his God; but when grief comes and sorrows overwhelm him, then will he remember his Father who is in heaven, and who is able to deliver him from his humiliations' (PT 50–1). He points out that:

'Men who suffer not, attain no perfections. The plant most pruned by the gardeners is that one which, when the summer comes, will have the most beautiful blossoms and the most abundant fruit' (Ibid.). But 'Abdu'l-Bahá goes on to say that:

> All the sorrow and the grief that exist come from the world of matter – the spiritual world bestows only the joy! If we suffer it is the outcome of material things, and all the trials and troubles come from this world of illusion.
>
> For instance, a merchant may lose his trade and depression ensues. A workman is dismissed and starvation stares him in the face. A farmer has a bad harvest, anxiety fills his mind. A man builds a house which is burnt to the ground and he is straightway homeless, ruined, and in despair.
>
> All these examples are to show you that the trials which beset our every step, all our sorrow, pain, shame and grief, are born in the world of matter; whereas the *spiritual kingdom* never causes sadness. A man living with his thoughts in *this Kingdom* knows perpetual joy. The ills all flesh is heir to *do not* pass him by, but they *only touch the surface* of his life, the depths are calm and serene.
>
> Today, humanity is bowed down with trouble, sorrow and grief, no one escapes; the world is wet with tears; but, thank God, the remedy is at our doors. Let us turn our hearts away from the world of matter and live in the spiritual world! It alone can give us freedom! If we are hemmed in by difficulties we have only to call upon God, and by His great Mercy we shall be helped. If sorrow and adversity visit us, let us turn our faces to *the Kingdom* and the heavenly consolation will be outpoured. (PT 110–11, emphasis added).

On a practical level, 'Abdu'l-Bahá's words help to show the relationship between being happy or blessed and being in the Kingdom of God. Blessedness is the fruit of the spiritual conditions which Bahá'u'lláh speaks of in verses XXIV:1–21. These are the conditions that bring happiness and constitute the Kingdom of God.

All these statements about the blessings of God involve recognition of and faith in Bahá'u'lláh, and spiritual transformation through following His teachings. They describe specific instances of what it means to enter the Kingdom, both the way to, and the blessings of, that spiritual condition. In the Beatitudes of Christ entrance into the Kingdom is expressed as being comforted, being filled with righteousness, obtaining mercy, seeing God, and becoming the child of God. Bahá'u'lláh's words unfold the same spiritual message for today. The one who has been awakened, quickened, solaced, and raised to life by His Revelation, who has testified to His truth, remained steadfast, is willing to suffer for Him, arises to teach His Faith, understands His Writings, practises His teachings, loves Him, and who stands firm in His covenant is a person who has gained admittance into His Kingdom. Such a person is a Bahá'í and is blessed – upon that person rests Bahá'u'lláh's mercy, His loving-kindness, His bounty, and His glory.

ABBREVIATIONS TO BIBLICAL AND BAHÁ'Í BOOKS CITED

THE HOLY BIBLE

KJV	King James Version (Authorized)
NIV	New International Version
NKJV	New King James Version
RV	Revised Standard Version

Old Testament Books

Gen.	Genesis
Exod.	Exodus
Lev.	Leviticus
1 Kgs.	1 Kings
Ps.	Psalms
Prov.	Proverbs
Isa.	Isaiah
Ezek.	Ezekiel
Zech.	Zechariah

New Testament Books

Matt.	Matthew
Rom.	Romans
1 Cor.	1 Corinthians
2 Cor.	2 Corinthians
Gal.	Galatians
Eph.	Ephesians
Phil.	Philippians
Col.	Colossians
1 Thess.	1 Thessalonians
2 Tim.	Timothy
Heb.	Hebrews
Jas.	James
1 Pet.	1 Peter
Rev.	Revelation

BAHÁ'Í BOOKS:

(For further information see the bibliography.)

Writings of the Báb:

SWB	Selections From the Writings of the Báb

Writings of Bahá'u'lláh:

ESW	Epistle to the Son of the Wolf
GWB	Gleanings From the Writings of Bahá'u'lláh
HWA	The Hidden Words of Bahá'u'lláh (from the Arabic)
KI	The Kitáb-i-Íqán: The Book of Certitude
PB	The Proclamation of Bahá'u'lláh
PM	Prayers and Meditations by Bahá'u'lláh
TB	Tablets of Bahá'u'lláh

Writings of 'Abdu'l-Bahá:

PT	Paris Talks
PUP	The Promulgation of Universal Peace
SAQ	Some Answered Questions
SDC	The Secret of Divine Civilization
SWA	Selections from the Writings of 'Abdu'l-Bahá

Writings of Shoghi Effendi

GPB	God Passes By
LGANZ	Letters from the Guardian to Australia and New Zealand
PDC	The Promised Day is Come
WOB	The World Order of Bahá'u'lláh

Other Bahá'í Books

BNE	Bahá'u'lláh and the New Era
BWF	Bahá'í World Faith
LG	Lights of Guidance

BIBLIOGRAPHY

'Abdu'l-Bahá, *Paris Talks, Addresses given by 'Abdu'l-Bahá in Paris in 1911–12*, London: Bahá'í Publishing Trust, 1912, 11th edn, 1969.
— *The Promulgation of Universal Peace: Talks Delivered by 'Abdu'l-Bahá During His Visit to the United States and Canada in 1912*, compiled by Howard MacNutt, Wilmette, Illinois: Bahá'í Publishing Trust, 1922–5, 2nd edn, 1982.
— *The Secret of Divine Civilization*, trans. Marzieh Gail and Ali-Kuli Khan, Wilmette, Illinois: Bahá'í Publishing Trust, 1957, 2nd edn, 1970.
— *Selections from the Writings of 'Abdu'l-Bahá*, compiled by the Research Department of the Universal House of Justice, trans. Marzieh Gail and a Committee at the Bahá'í World Centre, Haifa, Israel: Bahá'í World Centre, 1978.
— *Some Answered Questions*, collected and trans. Laura Clifford Barney, Wilmette, Illinois: Bahá'í Publishing Trust, 1908, 4th edn, 1964.
— *Tablets of the Divine Plan*, Wilmette, Illinois: Bahá'í Publishing Trust, 1959, 1975.
— *Will and Testament of 'Abdu'l-Bahá*, Wilmette, Illinois, Bahá'í Publishing Trust, 1944, 1971.
Báb, The, *Selections from the Writings of The Báb*, compiled by the Research Department of the Universal House of Justice, trans. Habib Taherzadeh and a committee at the Bahá'í World Centre, Haifa, Israel: Bahá'í World Centre, 1976.
Bahá'u'lláh, *Epistle To The Son Of The Wolf*, trans. Shoghi Effendi, Wilmette, Illinois: Bahá'í Publishing Trust, 1941, 3rd edn, 1976.
— *Gleanings from the Writings of Bahá'u'lláh*, trans. Shoghi Effendi, Wilmette, Illinois: Bahá'í Publishing Trust, 1939, 2nd edn, 1952.

— *The Hidden Words*, trans. Shoghi Effendi, Wilmette, Illinois: Bahá'í Publishing Trust, 1939; London: Oneworld Publications, 1986.

— *The Kitáb-i-Íqán: The Book of Certitude*, trans. Shoghi Effendi, Wilmette, Illinois: Bahá'í Publishing Trust, 1931, 3rd edn, 1974.

— *Prayers and Meditations by Bahá'u'lláh*, compiled and trans. Shoghi Effendi, London: Bahá'í Publishing Trust, 1957, 1978.

— *The Proclamation of Bahá'u'lláh*, Haifa, Israel: Bahá'í World Centre, 1972.

— *The Reality of Man: Excerpts From the Writings of Bahá'u'lláh and 'Abdu'l-Bahá*, Wilmette, Illinois: Bahá'í Publishing Trust, 1931, 2nd edn, 1962.

— *Synopsis and Codification of the Laws and Ordinances of the Kitáb-i-Aqdas*, trans. Shoghi Effendi, Haifa: Bahá'í World Centre, 1973.

— *Tablets of Bahá'u'lláh Revealed After the Kitáb-i-Aqdas*, compiled by the Research Department of the Universal House of Justice, trans. Habib Taherzadeh, and a Committee at the Bahá'í World Centre, Haifa, Israel: Bahá'í World Centre, 1978.

Balyuzi, H. M., *Bahá'u'lláh*, Oxford: George Ronald, 1963, 1974.

Barackman, Floyd H., *Practical Christian Theology*, Old Tappan, New Jersey: Fleming H. Revell Co., 1984.

Bausani, Alessandro, *The Persians*, trans. J. B. Donne, London: Elek Books, 1967.

Beckwith, I. T., *The Apocalypse of John*, New York: MacMillan, 1919.

The Holy Bible, Authorized King James Version, Glasgow: Collins, 1975.

The Holy Bible, New King James Version, Nashville, Tennessee: Thomas Nelson, 1982.

Browne, E. G., *A Literary History of Persia*, vol. IV, Cambridge: Cambridge University Press, 1924, 1953.

The Cambridge History of the Bible. vol. 1, From the Beginnings to Jerome, P. R. Ackroyd, and C. F. Evans, ed., Cambridge: Cambridge University Press, 1970.

Cohen, Daniel, *Waiting for the Apocalypse*, Buffalo, N.Y.: Prometheus Books, 1983.

Dewick, E. C., *The Christian Attitude to Other Religions*,

Cambridge: Cambridge University Press, 1953.
Durant, Will, *Caesar and Christ*, New York: Simon & Schuster, 1944.
Eban, Abba, *Heritage: Civilization and the Jews*, New York: Summit Books, 1984.
Effendi, Shoghi, *God Passes By*, Wilmette, Illinois: Bahá'í Publishing Trust, 1944, 2nd edn, 1974.
— *Letters from the Guardian to Australia and New Zealand, 1923–1957*, Sydney: National Spiritual Assembly of the Bahá'ís of Australia, 1970.
— *The Promised Day is Come*, Wilmette, Illinois: Bahá'í Publishing Trust, 1941, 2nd edn, 1980.
— *The World Order of Bahá'u'lláh: Selected Letters by Shoghi Effendi*, Wilmette, Illinois: Bahá'í Publishing Trust, 1938, 2nd edn, 1974.
The Encyclopedia of Islam, ed. Lewis, Menage, Pellat and Schacht, vol 3, Netherlands: Brill, 2nd edn, 1971.
The Encyclopedia of Religion, ed. Vergilius Ferm, Secaucus, N.J.: Poplar Books, 1945.
Encyclopedia of Religion and Ethics, ed. James Hastings, vols II and IV, New York: Charles Scribner's Sons.
Esslemont, J. E., *Bahá'u'lláh and the New Era*, Wilmette, Illinois: Bahá'í Publishing Trust, 1923, 5th edn, 1980.
Froom, LeRoy Edwin, *The Prophetic Faith of Our Fathers*, vols I–IV, Washington, D.C.: Review and Herald, 1950–4.
Gaebelein, Frank E., *Four Minor Prophets, Obadiah, Jonah, Habakkuk, and Haggai*, Chicago, Illinois: Moody Press, 1970.
Gibbon, Edward, *The Decline And Fall Of The Roman Empire*, 6 vols. 1776–88, abridged by D. M. Low, New York: Harcourt, Brace, 1960.
Graham, Billy, *Approaching Hoofbeats*, New York: Avon Books, 1983.
Guelich, Robert A., 'Interpreting the Sermon on the Mount', *Interpretation: A Journal of Bible and Theology*, vol. XLI, no. 2 (April 1987), Richmond, Virginia. Union Theological Seminary.
Harrison, J. F. C., *The Second Coming: Popular Millenarianism*, London: Routledge and Kegan Paul, 1979.
Henry, Carl F. H., ed., *Basic Christian Doctrines*, Grand Rapids, Michigan: Baker Book House, 1985.
Henry, Matthew, *Matthew Henry's Commentary on the Whole Bible*, Grand Rapids, Michigan: Zondervan Publishing

House, new one vol. edn., 1961.
Holley, Horace, ed., *Bahá'í Scriptures. Selections from the Utterances of Bahá'u'lláh and 'Abdu'l-Bahá*, New York: Brentano's, 1923; 2nd edn, 1928, New York Bahá'í Publishing Co.
Jonsson, Carl Olaf, and Herbst Wolfgang, *The Sign of the Last Days – When*, Atlanta, Georgia: Commentary Press, 1987.
Küng, Hans, *Christianity and the World Religions*, Garden City, New York: Doubleday, 1986.
Lachs, Samual Tobias, *A Rabbinic Commentary on the New Testament*, Hoboken, New Jersey: KTAV Publishing House, 1987.
Lange, John, *Commentary on the Holy Scriptures*, vol. 12, Grand Rapids, Michigan: Zondervan Publishing House, 1960.
Lights of Guidance: A Bahá'í Reference File, compiled by Helen Hornby, New Delhi, India: Bahá'í Publishing Trust, 1983.
Lindsey, Hal, *The Late Great Planet Earth*, Grand Rapids, Michigan: Zondervan Publishing House, 1970.
Martin, Alfred and Martin, John, *Isaiah: The Glory of the Messiah*, Chicago, Illinois: Moody Press, 1983.
Momen, Moojan, ed., *The Bábí and Bahá'í Religions, 1844–1944: Some Contemporary Western Accounts*, Oxford: George Ronald, 1981.
— *Selections from the Writings of E. G. Browne on the Bábí and Bahá'í Religions*, Oxford: George Ronald, 1987.
Nabíl-i-A'ẓam (Muḥammad-i-Zarandí) *The Dawn-Breakers, Nabíl's Narrative of the Early Days of the Bahá'í Revelation*, trans. and ed. Shoghi Effendi, Wilmette, Illinois: Bahá'í Publishing Trust, 1932, 1974.
New Bible Dictionary, Wheaton, Illinois: Tyndale House Publishers, 1962, 2nd edn, 1982.
The New Layman's Bible Commentary in One Volume, ed., G. C. D. Howley, F. F. Bruce and H. L. Ellison, Grand Rapids, Michigan: Zondervan Publishing House, 1979.
Parrinder, Geoffrey, *Avatar and Incarnation*, New York: Oxford University Press, 1970, 1982.
— *Jesus in the Qur'án*, New York: Oxford University Press, 1977.
Patte, Daniel, *The Gospel According to Matthew: A Structural Commentary on Matthew's Faith*, Philadelphia, Pennsylvania:

Fortress Press, 1978.
Powell, Ivor, *Matthew's Majestic Gospel*, Grand Rapids, Michigan: Kregel Publications, 1987.
The Holy Qur'án, trans. and commentary A. Yusuf Ali,: American Trust Publications, 1938, 2nd edn, 1977.
Richardson, Alan, ed., *A Theological Word Book of the Bible*, New York, N.Y.: MacMillan, 1950, 1978.
Ruhe, David S., *Door of Hope: A Century of the Bahá'í Faith in the Holy Land*, Oxford: George Ronald, 1983.
Sears, William, *The Wine of Astonishment*, Oxford: George Ronald, 1963, 2nd edn, 1974.
Taherzadeh, Adib, *The Revelation of Bahá'u'lláh*, Oxford: George Ronald, vol. I, 1974, 2nd edn, 1975; vol. II, 1977; vol. III, 1983; vol. IV, 1987.
Tan, Paul Lee, *The Interpretation of Prophecy*, Winona Lake, Indiana, Assurance Publishers: Ann Arbor, Michigan: Cushing-Malloy, 1974.
Trench, R. C., *Commentary on the Epistles to the Seven Churches in Asia*, Kegan Paul, Trench, Trubner, 1987; Minneapolis, Minnesota: Klock and Klock Christian Publishers, 6th edn, 1978.
Universal House of Justice, *Wellspring of Guidance: Messages from the Universal House of Justice 1963–1968*, Wilmette, Illinois: Bahá'í Publishing Trust, 1969.
Vine, W. E., *Vine's Expository Dictionary of Biblical Words*, Nashville, Thomas Nelson, 1985.
White, John Wesley, *Re-entry*, Minneapolis, Minnesota: World Wide Publications, 1971.
Woodruff, William, *Impact of Western Man*, New York: St. Martin's Press, 1967. (Excerpted in *The Modern Era: 1815 to the Present*, ed. Norman F. Cantor and Samuel Berner, New York: Thomas Y. Crowell, 1971.)

INDEX TO BIBLE REFERENCES

Gen. 2:7, p. 158
Gen. 6:17, p. 158
Gen. 22:1, p. 74
Gen. 22:7, p. 74
Gen. 22:11, p. 74

Exod. 3:4, p. 74
Exod. 21–23, p. 184
Exod. 24, p. 184
Exod. 24:16, p. 74
Exod. 26, p. 137
Exod. 32, p. 139
Exod. 34:29–30, p. 137
Exod. 35–40, p. 164n
Exod. 40:27, p. 134
Exod. 40:34, p. 161

Lev. 1:9, p. 134
Lev. 1:13, p. 134
Lev. 1:17, p. 134

Deut. 4:2, p. 99

1 Kgs. 8:27, p. 31

Ps. 11:4, p. 31
Ps. 24:3–5, p. 68
Ps. 68:8, p. 134n
Ps. 105:15, p. 36
Ps. 111:10, p. 63n
Ps. 118:22, p. 106
Ps. 139:7–10, p. 10

Isa. 2, p. 155
Isa. 2:2, p. 156n

Isa. 2:3, p. 99, 156n, 162
Isa. 4:5–6, p. 164, 170
Isa. 4:6, p. 162n
Isa. 7:14, p. 38
Isa. 8:14, p. 106
Isa. 9:6, p. 38, 130
Isa. 9:6–7, p. 43, 76–7
Isa. 11:9, p. 73
Isa. 24:15, p. 187n
Isa. 28:5, p. 178
Isa. 28:16, p. 106
Isa. 33:17, p. 160
Isa. 35:2, p. 37, 128
Isa. 38:18–19, p. 182
Isa. 40:3, p. 94
Isa. 40:5, p. 37, 128
Isa. 42:8, p. 139
Isa. 44:18, p. 139
Isa. 44:20, p. 139
Isa. 45:1, p. 36
Isa. 46:10, p. 30
Isa. 49:6, p. 167
Isa. 57:15, p. 31
Isa. 60:1, p. 157
Isa. 61:1, p. 36, 57n
Isa. 61:2, p. 36
Isa. 65:25, p. 87
Isa. 66:16, p. 43

Ezek. 43:2, p. 37, 128

Haggai 2:7, p. 55–6n

Zech. 6:12, p. 161n, 162n, 163n
Zech. 14:12, p. 60n

INDEX TO BIBLE REFERENCES 199

Matt. 1:23, p. 38
Matt. 2:3–6, p. 43, 44
Matt. 3:3, p. 94
Matt. 4:10, p. 51
Matt. 4:18, p. 48
Matt. 4:24, p. 125
Matt. 5:3, p. 54n, 154, 187
Matt. 5:3–5, p. 152
Matt. 5:6, p. 164
Matt. 5–7, p. 153n
Matt. 5:8, p. 68
Matt. 5:10, p. 154, 181, 187
Matt. 5:11, p. 157, 181
Matt. 5:20, p. 154
Matt. 5:45, p. 149
Matt. 6:24, p. 54n
Matt. 7:21, p. 154
Matt. 8:20, p. 169
Matt. 8:21–2, p. 146
Matt. 8:22, p. 110n
Matt. 9:16, p. 134
Matt. 10:34, p. 44
Matt. 10:38, p. 143
Matt. 10:38–9, p. 65
Matt. 11:15, p. 103
Matt. 11:19, p. 137n
Matt. 11:25, p. 49
Matt. 12:28, p. 69
Matt. 12:33–7, p. 106
Matt. 13:9, p. 103
Matt. 13:13–15, p. 103–4
Matt. 13:43, p. 103
Matt. 16:16, p. 51
Matt. 16:18, p. 106
Matt. 19:12, p. 54n
Matt. 19:21, p. 54n
Matt. 20:16, p. 167
Matt. 21:42, p. 106
Matt. 22:37, p. 96
Matt. 23:13, p. 141
Matt. 24, p. 64, 74, 114, 177
Matt. 24:3, p. 177
Matt. 24:24, p. 95n
Matt. 24:26–7, p. 174
Matt. 24:27, p. 111
Matt. 24:29, p. 113
Matt. 24:30, p. 40, 106, 128, 173, 174n
Matt. 24:31, p. 81n

Matt. 24:42–4, p. 69n
Matt. 25, p. 121, 177
Matt. 25:31, p. 81n, 106, 128
Matt. 25:31–2, p. 121
Matt. 25:31–46, p. 116
Matt. 25:34, p. 120
Matt. 25:37, p. 121
Matt. 25:41, p. 122
Matt. 25:46, p. 122
Matt. 25:57, p. 51
Matt. 26:63–7, p. 44, 51

Mark 1:5–10, p. 74
Mark 1:19–20, p. 48
Mark 2:3–12, p. 43
Mark 2:21, p. 134
Mark 8:36, p. 80
Mark 8:38, p. 37, 61, 76, 128
Mark 13:26, p. 37, 128
Mark 13:31, p. 115
Mark 13:32, p. 81
Mark 14:24, p. 184
Mark 15:38, p. 138

Luke 1:17, p. 115
Luke 1:32, p. 44
Luke 1:78, p. 47n
Luke 3:8, p. 106
Luke 4:18, p. 57n
Luke 4:18–19, p. 36, 44, 96
Luke 5:1–10, p. 48
Luke 5:18–25, p. 43
Luke 5:27, p. 49
Luke 10:19, p. 108
Luke 10:20, p. 107
Luke 11:2, p. 69
Luke 11:52, p. 141
Luke 13:24, p. 87
Luke 13:24–30, p. 187n
Luke 17:20–1, p. 44, 87, 156
Luke 19:39–40, p. 106
Luke 21:33, p. 115
Luke 22:29–30, p. 165
John 1:1, p. 77n
John 1:11, p. 77
John 1:12–13, p. 77n, 130
John 1:14, p. 77n
John 1:29, p. 37
John 1:36, p. 37

John 1:42, p. 106
John 2:19–21, p. 163, 163n
John 3:3, p. 95
John 3:13, p. 40
John 3:19, p. 47n
John 4:10, p. 74
John 5:22, p. 116
John 5:23, p. 45
John 5:24, p. 95
John 5:46, p. 58
John 6:38, p. 30–1, 40, 69
John 6:41, p. 41
John 6:41–2, p. 70
John 6:51, p. 166
John 6:63, p. 59, 63
John 7:17, p. 80
John 7:38, p. 74
John 7:45–9, p. 45
John 8:19, p. 45
John 8:31–2, p. 80
John 9:5, p. 39n, 79, 114n, 129
John 10:4, p. 10n
John 10:16, p. 76
John 12:12–13, p. 43
John 12:49, p. 31, 100
John 14:7, p. 45, 130
John 14:15–16, p. 84
John 14:26, p. 83
John 15:13, p. 60
John 15:16, p. 167
John 15:26, p. 83
John 16, p. 74
John 16:7–15, p. 83–4
John 16:12, p. 78, 84
John 16:13, p. 99, 100
John 16:14–15, p. 82, 100
John 18:12–14, p. 49
John 18:14, p. 51
John 18:36, p. 44, 156n
John 18:37, p. 44
John 19:10–11, p. 116
John 19:34, p. 174

Acts 2, p. 83
Acts 4:12, p. 38
Acts 4:13, p. 51
Acts 7:49, p. 44
Acts 9:1, p. 180
Acts 9:4, p. 180
Acts 10:36, p. 44
Acts 10:38, p. 36
Acts 20:29, p. 64

Rom. 1:19–20, p. 131
Rom. 5:8, p. 60
Rom. 8:9, p. 42
Rom. 8:14, p. 130
Rom. 10:17, p. 95

1 Cor. 1:22–4, p. 71, 142
1 Cor. 1:22–5, p. 138
1 Cor. 5:11, p. 139
1 Cor. 6:9, p. 120
1 Cor. 7:7, p. 54n
1 Cor. 7:25–6, p. 54n
1 Cor. 7:32–5, p. 54n
1 Cor. 10:21, p. 165
1 Cor. 12:3, p. 102
1 Cor. 12:12–13, p. 180
1 Cor. 12:27, p. 71, 180
1 Cor. 15:14, p. 71
1 Cor. 15:50, p. 96

2 Cor. 2:15, p. 134n
2 Cor. 3:14–15, p. 138
2 Cor. 5:17, p. 89, 132
2 Cor. 6:16, p. 163
2 Cor. 10:3–5, p. 44

Gal. 1:8f, p. 98n
Gal. 4:24, p. 75
Gal. 4:24–6, p. 134
Gal. 5:19–20, p. 139

Eph. 1:18, p. 159, 173–4
Eph. 2:4–6, p. 89
Eph. 2:5, p. 181
Eph. 2:19, p. 128
Eph. 2:8, p. 95
Eph. 5:2, p. 135n
Eph. 5:5, p. 139
Eph. 5:19, p. 182
Eph. 6:17, p. 44

Phil. 4:18, p. 135n

Col. 1:6, p. 132
Col. 1:23, p. 132

INDEX TO BIBLE REFERENCES

Col. 3:5, p. 139

1 Thess. 2:19, p. 178
1 Thess. 4:13–17, p. 109, 181
1 Thess. 4:13–18, p. 110n
1 Thess. 4:16–17, p. 187n

1 Tim. 3:1–7, p. 113n

2 Tim. 1:10, p. 131
2 Tim. 3:16, p. 158

Heb. 9, p. 162n
Heb. 9:11, p. 163
Heb. 9:22–8, p. 184
Heb. 12:23, p. 107
Heb. 13:8, p. 38

Jas. 1:12, p. 178
Jas. 2:26, p. 81, 110n
Jas. 5:7–9, p. 68

1 Pet. 1:23, p. 77n, 95
1 Pet. 2:4–5, p. 106
1 Pet. 2:5, p. 128
1 Pet. 2:6–8, p. 106
1 Pet. 3:18, p. 60
1 Pet. 5:4, p. 178

1 John 3:6, p. 81
1 John 3:24, p. 81

1 John 4:1–2, p. 101

Rev. 1:7, p. 173, 174
Rev. 2:9, p. 169n
Rev. 2:17, p. 39
Rev. 2:26, p. 108
Rev. 3:12, p. 39
Rev. 3:17, p. 169n
Rev. 3:19, p. 74n
Rev. 5:12, p. 142
Rev. 11–12, p. 151n
Rev. 19, p. 151, 174
Rev. 19–22, p. 151n
Rev. 19:6, p. 30
Rev. 19:13, p. 38, 39
Rev. 19:15, p. 97
Rev. 19:16, p. 39, 151n
Rev. 19:21, p. 60n
Rev. 20–21, p. 155
Rev. 20:15, p. 107
Rev. 21, p. 187n
Rev. 21:1, p. 162n
Rev. 21:3, p. 162, 162n
Rev. 21:3–5, p. 131
Rev. 21:4, p. 88
Rev. 21:6, p. 164
Rev. 21:7, p. 120
Rev. 21:22, p. 162n
Rev. 21:23, p. 37, 128
Rev. 22:1, p. 187n
Rev. 22:17, p. 164, 187n

GENERAL INDEX

Aaron, 137
'Abdu'l-Bahá, 8, 60, 81n, 183
  Centre of the Covenant, 185
  explanation of 'arisen from the dead', 181–2
  explanation of 'clouds of heaven', 40, 70
  explanation of 'the wolf and the lamb', 87–8
  grandson of, see Shoghi Effendi
  mentioned, 7n, 38n, 66n, 151n
  on the attributes of God, 86
  on believers, 172
  on the 'chosen ones', 166, 167
  on Christ, 61–2, 70, 79, 115n, 158n
  on Christianity and the Bahá'í Faith, 99
  on the differences between people, 167–8
  on the equalization of wealth, 123–4
  on the Kingdom of God, 165–6, 171–2
  on the poor, 153n
  on progressive revelation, 62, 79
  on religion as a means of love and fellowship, 122
  on response of the Western world to the East, 112n
  on the Spirit of Truth, 83
  on suffering, 188–90
  on the teachings of Bahá'u'lláh, 91–2
  Will and Testament of, 185
Abhá, 165
Abraham, 106
Abu'l-Faḍl, Mírzá, 76–7
Administrative Order, Bahá'í, 112, 155, 156n, 185–6
Adrianople (Edirne), 5
Adventist movement, 58
Afnán, 185
Aghṣán, 185
Aḥmad Big Tawfíq, 66n
'Akká, 6, 18, 65–6, 74n
Alexander II, Czar, 6
'Alí-Muḥammad, Siyyid (the Báb), 5
America, 8, 58, 112
Andrew, 48, 172
angels, 19, 81n, 107n
animals, sacrifice of, 134, 162n, 184
'Anointed, the', 36
anti-Christ, 151n
Apostles, 44, 48–9, 71, 83, 98, 177
aqueduct ('Akká), 66n
Arabic language, 7, 13n, 74n, 129n, 150n, 170n, 176
Ark of the Covenant, 137n, 162
assistance, 34
Austro-Hungary, 6, 119

Báb, the ('the Gate'), 5, 93–4, 97, 111, 186

GENERAL INDEX

foretells coming of
  Bahá'u'lláh, 5
Bábí Faith, 93, 142, 186
Bábís, 5, 94, 141
Ba<u>gh</u>dád, 5, 141
Bahá, 165n
Bahá'í Era, 58
Bahá'í Faith, 5, 9, 12, 58
  Administrative Order of, 112
  covenant of the, 184–6
  defence of, by Bahá'u'lláh, 35
  devotion to, 187
  divinely ordained, 140
  humble people recognize,
    106–7
  in America and England, 112
  investigation of, for oneself,
    20–1, 103, 174
  no priesthood in, 98
  opposition to, 122–3, 148
  persecution of, 181
  reception of, in Iran, 8
  relationship to Christianity,
    10, 102
  role of Christians in
    spreading, 8
  same as Christian Faith, 98–9,
    115–16, 132
  spreading the (teaching), 98,
    108, 147–9, 180
  teachings of, see teachings of
    Bahá'u'lláh
  triumph of, 61
  unity of, 185–6
  violence forbidden in, 148,
    179
Bahá'í World Centre, 37n, 58,
  156
Bahá'ís, 7, 8, 130–2, 188, 190
  'chosen ones', 166–7
  enjoined to teach the Faith,
    147–9
  independent investigation of
    truth, 98
  interpretation of Scripture, 11
  persecution of, 121, 141–2,
    180–1
  Western, 112

Bahá'u'lláh, 5
  acceptance of, 136, 157
  affirms that Jesus is the Christ,
    102
  attitude to, 66n
  authority of, 17, 29
  bearing witness to, 23, 130–2
  biblical signs of truth of, 101
  birth of, 59
  Cause of, see Bahá'í Faith
  and Christ, 19, 57, 82–4
  claims of, 30–1, 59, 62, 67, 69
    acknowledgement of, 33
    Messianic nature of, 32,
      57–8, 68, 128
    objections to, 81
    set out to world rulers, 6
    truth of, 57, 85
  coming foretold by the Báb, 5,
    94
  companions of, 6
  Covenant of, 184–6
  cultural background of, 9
  dialogue with Bethlehem,
    22–3, 127–30
  dialogue with Mount Sinai,
    23, 133–5
  divinely ordained advent of,
    79
  exile of, 5, 6, 58, 85, 129, 141,
    144, 172
  'the Father', 19, 23, 75–7, 130
  followers of, see Bahá'ís
  fulfilment of Messianic
    expectations, 8, 58
    see also prophecies, biblical
  'Glad-Tidings' of, 8, 98
  glorifies Christ, 20, 82, 96, 101
  glory of, 22, 128–9, 145–6,
    161, 190
  'Glory of God', 36–7, 39, 129
  Greatest Name, 21, 77, 105
  'Him Whom God Shall Make
    Manifest', 93n, 94
  imprisonment of, 5, 6, 18, 20,
    65–6, 89, 129, 141, 144, 172
  interpretation of Bible, 10–11

Kingdom of God on earth
  ushered in by, 155
leadership of Bábís, 5
leads followers to truth, 100
life of, 145
'Life-Giver of the World', 24,
  145, 146
mission of, 31, 32, 58
name of, 36–41
opposition to, 23, 36–42, 44,
  60, 69, 81, 116, 140–2, 175
passing of, 6
power of, 61
proof that He is a
  Manifestation, 94–5
prophecies concerning, 55n
recognition of, 23, 130, 157,
  177
re-establishment of the ancient
  Faith of God, 125
on miracles, 95–6
on the true seeker, 104
rejection of, 53–4
relationship to God, 160
religious heritage of, 9
return of Christ, 8, 58, 115,
  128, 151n
Revelation of, see Revelation
  of Bahá'u'lláh
sacrifice of, 58–60, 97, 128,
  129, 145, 172–3
same Spirit as Christ, 19,
  67–8, 115
same spiritual message as
  Christ's, 152, 154, 156, 190
Shrine of, 30n
Spirit of Truth, 20, 99–100,
  180
station of, 187
successor of, see 'Abdu'l-Bahá
sufferings of, 8, 18, 23,
  60–1, 65–6, 85, 89–91,
  143–4, 145–6, 179
summons people to God, 85–6
supporter of the Báb, 5
tablets of, to kings and rulers,
  5–6
teachings of, see teachings of
  Bahá'u'lláh

titles of, 17, 31, 36, 54–6,
  151n
use of biblical Scripture and
  terminology, 9–11, 67
use of metaphorical and
  symbolic language, 11, 158
veils to recognition of, 136–40
willingness to suffer as Christ
  did, 116
writings of, see writings of
  Bahá'u'lláh
Bausani, Alessandro, 141
Bayán, the, 20, 93–4
Beatitudes, the, 152–4, 156, 157,
  187, 190
beauty, 24, 159–60
believer, 147, 151, 156, 171, 172
Bethlehem, 22–3, 126, 127–30
Bible, 9, 12, 13, 31
  Bahá'u'lláh's interpretation of,
    10–11
  confirms claims of
    Bahá'u'lláh, 75
  interpretation of, 64
  multiple meanings, 40
  proof of Manifestation, 95
  prophecies of the, see
    prophecies, biblical
  signs of truth of Bahá'u'lláh,
    101
  symbolism of, 30
bishops, 22, 105, 113–15
blessedness, state of, 24, 152–90
'bread', 128, 166
'breath', 24, 25, 158–9, 171
'Breeze of God', 21, 22, 108, 109,
  111, 127
Browne, E. G., 93n, 142
Bruce, Reverend Dr Robert, 76–7
Buddhists, 88
Burning Bush, 19, 73, 75, 138
Buzurg, Mírzá, 59

Catholic Church, 118, 119
Caiaphas, 51
Carmel, 37
  Mount Carmel, 37n, 58, 156n
certitude, 181–2
chastisement, Divine, 6

GENERAL INDEX

'chosen ones', 24, 165, 166–7
Christ, 8, 10n, 30, 36
   Bahá'í Faith teaches that Jesus is the, 102
   and Bahá'u'lláh, 19, 57, 82–4
   Bahá'u'lláh same Spirit as, 19, 67–8, 115
   baptism of, 74
   'but you cannot bear them now', 19, 78
   called Immanuel, 38
   the chief cornerstone, 106
   claims of, 44, 69
   crucifixion of, 114, 138, 143–4, 163n, 184
   death of, for our sins, 60
   defines 'the dead', 146
   discourses of, 10
   established a new covenant, 184
   example of, 43
   as example of real wealth, 169
   and forces of evil, 60
   foretold Spirit of Truth, 99
   fulfilment of prophecy, 44n, 46–7, 52, 175
   glorified by Bahá'u'lláh, 20, 82, 101
   healing performed by, 96
   influence of, 50, 115n
   leads followers to truth, 100
   miracles of, 95–6
   names of, 37–41
   objections to, 41, 42, 49
   piercing of, while on Cross, 174
   poverty of, 169
   power of, 62
   prophecies of, 61, 72, 74, 78, 80, 101, 111, 113–14
   reality of, 38n
   recognition of, 49, 50–2, 89, 157
   rejection of, a rejection of God, 45–6
   rejection of, by Pharisees and Jews, 42–53, 70, 163n, 167
   resurrection of, 70–2
   return of, 8, 37–41, 53, 58, 61–2, 71–2, 81–2, 87, 99–100, 106, 109, 113, 142, 151n, 155, 156n, 173–8
   in glory, 128
   Revelation of, 73–4
   sacrifice of, 60–1, 82, 142, 184
   second coming of, see Christ, return of
   sentenced to death, 18, 50
   'the Son', 19, 20, 73, 74, 101
   'the Spirit', 17, 18, 42, 53, 74
   spiritual message same as that of Bahá'u'lláh, 152, 154, 156
   spiritual sovereignty of, 173
   sufferings of, 22, 60–1, 65, 115–16, 142, 169, 175
   summons people to God, 85
   teachings of, 153
   title of, 36, 37–8
   trial of, 51
   as 'Word of God', 38
Christianity, 39n
   accepted by Constantine, 5n
   crisis in, 117–19
   decline of, 118–19
   persecution of, 144, 181
   recognition of, 49–50
   relationship to Bahá'í Faith, 10, 98–9
   revival of, 127
   spirit of, 115
   traditions of, 30n, 78
   triumph of, 143–4
Christians, 88, 93n, 134
   Bahá'u'lláh's warnings to, 69, 80, 90–1
   called to God, 129
   faithful, to inherit the Kingdom of God, 120
   'followers of the Son', 17, 35
   investigate truth of Bahá'u'lláh, 62, 63, 66
   Messianic expectations of, 8, 58
   objections to Bahá'u'lláh, 36–41, 42, 44, 69, 78, 81
   recognition of Bahá'u'lláh, 23, 130

role of, in spreading Bahá'í Faith, 8
spread of the Gospel, 131n
understanding Bahá'í interpretation, 11
Christians, Tablet to, see Tablet to the Christians
Church, the, 21, 64, 71, 80, 105, 113n, 117, 128, 163
    Catholic, 118, 119
    crisis in, 117–19
clergy
    Christian, see priests
    Islamic, 5, 141
commandments, 96
Constantine, 5n
Constantinople (Istanbul), 5
'Court of holiness', 25, 183–4
covenant, 25, 75, 125, 133–5, 183–6
    Ark of the, 137n
    breaking the covenant, 185
    establishment of a new, 154, 156
    faithfulness and obedience to, 25, 168, 183, 185, 190
creation, 131–2
Cross, the, 138, 143, 162n
'crown', 178–9
Crucifixion, 114, 138, 143–4, 163n, 184

Damascus, 180
'day', 39n
Day of Reckoning (Day of Judgement), 22, 116–17, 177
'Dayspring', 45, 47, 47n, 172
dead, the (spiritually), 21, 24, 25, 108–10, 145–6, 181–2
deeds, good, 123
Deliverer, 55
'Desire of All Nations', 55–6
detachment, 25, 65, 187–8
'diadem', 25, 178–9
divines, 63
dominion, 43
Durant, Will, 10n

earth, spiritual explanation of, 148

East, the, 21, 111, 112n
Edirne (Adrianople), 5
Elijah, 37n, 115
eternity, 31
Europe, 8, 50, 112
Evangel, the, 18, 57
    see also New Testament
evil, 60, 133
Exodus, 161–3

faith, 10, 46, 95, 134–5, 146, 158, 167, 168, 184
    in Bahá'u'lláh, 190
    life of, 25, 89, 139, 146, 159, 171–2
    steadfastness of, 24, 147–9
Faris Effendi, 6–7
Father, the, 19, 23, 75–7, 130
'followers of the Son', see Christians
Franz-Josef, Emperor, 6

Genesis, 158
Gentiles, 167
Germany, 58
Glad-Tidings, 8, 98
glory, 24–5, 32, 36–7, 91–2, 128–9, 138, 142, 145–6, 161, 168–9, 173, 187
God, 10, 17, 29, 37
    assistance of, 34
    attributes of, 86, 131
    authority of, 85
    Bahá'u'lláh's relationship to, 160
    covenant of, see covenant
    as creator, 148
    duty to, 85–6
    eternity of, 31
    faithfulness to, 116
    'the Father', 19, 75–7
    fear of, 18, 63
    Glory of, see Bahá'u'lláh
    goodness of, 164
    Kingdom of, see Kingdom of God
    knowledge of, 188
        is only through Prophets, 45
    love of, 25, 60, 169–70, 172, 178–9

GENERAL INDEX

names of, 17, 33, 37
nature of, 31
power of, 142, 148–9, 172
presence of, 176–8
reality of, 30, 31
recognition of, 49
rejection of Christ a rejection of God, 45–6
relation of mankind to, 34, 100
Revelation of, *see* Revelation of God
spiritual protection of, 164
word of, *see* 'Word of God'
golden rule, 153
Gospel, 57, 58n, 73, 98, 134
  genuineness of, 82–3
  to be preached to the nations, 105, 131n, 132
  see also New Testament
government, 49, 77
  Islamic, 141
Graham, Billy, 88n, 89n
Greatest Name, 21, 77, 105
Greek Orthodox Church, 118
Greeks, 8, 142
Guardian of the Bahá'í Faith, *see* Shoghi Effendi
guidance, 34

Hands of the Cause of God, 185
happiness, 23, 136, 139, 153, 188–90
hardship, 180–1
Haydar-'Alí, Ḥájí Mírzá, 7n
heaven, 17, 22, 31–2, 113–14, 126
  clouds of, 40
  kingdom of, 187
  spiritual reality of, 40, 70, 132, 148
Hebrew, 56n, 74n
Hell, 182n
Henry, Matthew, 164–5, 174
Hezekiah, 182
'Him Whom God Shall Make Manifest', *see* Bahá'u'lláh
Holy Spirit, 59, 83, 102, 181–2
'holy vale', 74n

'house', 128
House, Lord's, 19, 73, 75
human nature, 62
humankind, 33
  advancement of, 181–2
  covenant with God, 133–5
  differences among, 167–8
  love of God for, 60
  obligations of, 184
  oneness of, 76, 77
  qualities of, 34
  relation to God, 34, 100
  relation to itself, 100
  station of, 34
  see also man
Ḥusayn, Imam, 109n

idolatry, 23, 139–40
interpretation, 11–12, 46, 66, 81–2, 87, 175–6
Iran *see* Persia
Isaiah, 88, 93, 139
  book of, 17–18, 36, 99, 182
  refers to future Messiah, 38, 46, 75–7, 130, 160, 167, 175
Islam, 9, 12, 30n, 140–2, 151n
  traditions of, 137
Islamic Revolution, 142
Israel, 37n, 51n, 58, 65, 129, 156n
Israelites, 184
Istanbul (Constantinople), 5

James, 48, 67–8, 178
Jerusalem, New, 162n
Jesus, *see* Christ
Jews, 8, 42n, 88, 134, 137, 142, 163n
  'chosen ones', 166
  expectation of the Messiah, 43, 44, 52
  idolatry, concept of, 139
  rejection of Christ, 23, 52, 70, 130, 163n, 167
John, 48, 98, 101, 116, 130, 172
John the Baptist, 73, 93–4, 115
Jordan, river, 19, 73–4
Joshua, 74n
Judaism, 9, 163n

traditions of, 30n
judgement of God, 116–17
justice, 6, 55

Ka'ba (the House of God), 30n
'Kibla (Qiblah) of the world', 30n
Kingdom of God, 19, 25, 67, 69, 75–6, 94, 117, 120–2, 126, 151, 165–6, 171–2, 177, 187–90
  on earth, 155–6
  at heart of Bahá'u'lláh's message, 154–6
kings, 5, 6
Kitáb-i-Aqdas (The Most Holy Book), 99
Kitáb-i-Íqán (The Book of Certitude), 7, 43, 55, 114, 137, 177
knowledge, 24, 100, 170–1
  of God, 188

Lambden, Stephen, 74n, 129n, 150n, 165n, 176n
law of God, 75, 99, 154, 156n, 162
Lawḥ-i-Aqdas (The Most Holy Tablet), see Tablet to the Christians
Lawḥ-i-Sulṭán, 6
laws of Bahá'u'lláh, 137
leaders
  of religion, 48–9, 64, 91, 103, 114, 117
  see also bishops, monks, Pharisees and priests
League of Militant Atheists, 118
liberty, 33, 89
life, 25, 158, 171–2, 190
  dedication of one's, 25, 180–1
  spiritual, 187, 188–90
'Lord', 34
  see also God
Lord's Prayer, 153
love, 60, 88, 142, 167, 181
  of God, 25, 169–70, 178–9, 187
Luke, 98

man, 158
  two natures of, 150–1
  see also humankind
Manifestations (Messengers, Prophets), 10, 34, 38n, 156n
  appearance of, 163n
  biblical criteria for discerning, 101–2
  call humankind back to God, 126, 139
  characteristics of, 85, 89
  lead followers to truth, 100
  progressive revelation, 55n
  proof of, 94–5
  provide knowledge of God, 43, 170–1, 177–8
  recognition of, 48, 49
  rejection of, 103
  revelation through, 131
  sacrifice of, 59, 142
  sent in every age, 62
  signs at appearance of, 114
  spiritual reality of, 36
  sufferings of, 89–90, 142, 169
  as the Word of God, 77n
mankind, see humankind
Mark, 98
marriage, 54n
martyrdom, 65n, 180–1
Mary, 70
Matthew, 48–9, 98, 114, 121, 154, 156
'melodies', 25, 182–3
Messenger of God, see Manifestations
Messiah, 36, 38, 40, 55, 76, 172, 175
  Jews' expectation of, 43, 91
Messianic expectations, 8, 53, 58
metaphors, explanation of, 79, 137, 157, 158, 168
Miller, William, 58
miracles, 95–6
missions, Christian, 50n
monasticism, 54
monks, 18, 53–6, 57, 105
  Bahá'u'lláh addresses, 22, 120–4
  compared to Pharisees, 53–4

GENERAL INDEX

marriage of, 54n
Moses, 57n, 58, 74n, 75, 137, 138, 139, 154, 162
  established covenant, 184
Most Great Name, see Greatest Name
Most Great Peace, 60
Most Holy Tablet, The (Lawh-i-Aqdas), see Tablet to the Christians
Mount Carmel, 37n, 58, 156n
Muḥammad, 42n, 58n, 100, 114
Murád, 24, 150
music, 182–3
Muslims, 9, 23, 30n, 88, 93n, 140–2

names, 17
  of Bahá'u'lláh, 36–41
  of God, 22, 86n, 116
  of Prophets, 36
Napoleon III, 6
Napoleonic Empire, 118
Náṣiri'd-Dín Sháh, 6, 23, 143
needy, the, 121–2, 123–4, 153n, 169
Nestorians, 88
New Testament, 44, 98, 99, 101–2, 110, 128, 134n, 153, 176
  cultural environment of, 9
  refers to the 'glory of God', 37
  terminology of, 137–8, 139
  use of earlier Scriptures, 10
  'night', 39n

Old Testament, 10, 11, 37, 137–8, 166
  prophecies of, 46, 128
  terminology of, 67n, 74, 134n, 137, 161
  warning against adding to the word of God, 99
Ottoman Empire, 129

Palestine, 129
parables, 103–4
Parousia, 176–7
  see also Christ, return of

Patte, Daniel, 154
Paul, 60, 64, 71, 75, 89, 102, 109–10, 120, 132, 137, 142, 158–9, 180
  warning regarding other gospels, 98–9
peace, 77, 124, 155
Pentateuch, 57n
perception, spiritual, 159–60, 171–6, 187
persecution, 141–2, 144, 145, 180–1
Persia (Iran), 5, 8, 94, 111, 112, 129, 141, 142, 181n
  Bahá'u'lláh's letter to ruler of, 6, 23, 143
Peter, 38, 44, 51, 60, 95, 172, 178
  name of, 106
Pharisees, 8, 17, 42, 43–50, 64, 70, 71, 91, 106, 172
  monks compared to, 53–4
Pilate, 116
pilgrims, 156n
Pius IX, Pope, 9, 118
Pontius Pilate, 51n
poor, the, see needy, the
prayers, 30n
'presence', 25, 176–8
priests, 20, 21, 54n, 62, 79, 80, 97–8, 105–8
  see also monks
Prince of Peace, 77
Promised Day is Come, The, 7
prophecies
  biblical, 7, 32, 40, 76, 99, 128, 157, 176
  Bahá'u'lláh's fulfilment of, 39, 72, 75, 78, 83–4, 88–9, 97, 100, 101, 106, 160, 170, 173–4
  Christ's fulfilment of, 46–7, 52
  concerning Immanuel, 38
  importance of heeding, 80
  interpretation of, 46, 81–2, 87, 175–6
  testimony of, 94–5, 97

of Christ, 61, 72, 74, 78, 111, 113–14
concerning the return of Christ, 58, 81–2, 106, 174
of earlier Scriptures, 57
fulfilment of, 57, 62, 73, 87–9, 111–12, 137, 156
literal interpretations of, 175
spiritual significance of, 89
Prophets, of Israel, 85
see also Manifestations
Prussia, 6

Qur'án, 9, 10, 13, 23, 65n, 140
terminology of, 67n, 86n, 176n

religion, 63
all religions come from the same source, 76, 132
decline of, 163n
followers of, 23, 143–4
leaders of, 48–9, 64, 91, 103, 117
must be the means of love and fellowship, 122–3
unity of, 88
renunciation, 187–8
resurrection, 108–10
see also Christ, resurrection of
revelation, 131
progressive, 55n, 79
Revelation, Book of, 11, 39, 84, 88–9, 142, 164, 174
Revelation of Bahá'u'lláh, 8, 11, 20, 78, 97, 164, 188
beauty of, 159
'Breeze of God', 21, 24, 108, 109, 111, 157
divine nature of, 19, 69
guidance of, 178
inspiration of, 159
oneness of, with the Revelation of Christ, 73
personal commitment to, 157
power of, 149
spiritual message of, 98
spread from East to West, 21, 111

understanding of, 159
Revelation of God, 33, 55, 74, 134, 138, 148
likened to music, 182–3
transcendent nature of, 31
reward, spiritual, 107, 153
righteousness, 149, 153, 156, 190
Romans, 5n, 51n
Russia, Soviet, 118

sacrifice, 59, 134–5, 142, 143, 162
animal, 134, 162n, 184
salvation, 164
Scriptures, the, 34, 186
authority of, 10
confirm claims of Bahá'u'lláh, 75
earlier, used as basis of theological argument, 10
Hebrew, 68
influence of cultural environment on, 9
interpretation of, 11–12, 46, 66
meaning of, 64
of past religions, 5
reverence for, 123
spiritual melodies of, 182–3
spiritual significance of, 72
students of, 47, 54, 98
symbolism of, 175–6
testify to Bahá'u'lláh, 84
understanding of, 48, 57
use of metaphor in, 79
see also Bible; writings of Bahá'u'lláh
seeker, 164, 165
true, 104, 126
selflessness, 60
Sermon on the Mount, 153–6
service, 60
Sháh of Persia, see Náṣiri'd-Dín Sháh
Sharon, 37
Shi'ites, 88, 141
Shiraz, 94

GENERAL INDEX

Shoghi Effendi, 8, 12n, 39n, 55n, 99, 151n, 168
  appointed Guardian of the Bahá'í Faith, 185
  interpretation of current events, 117–18
  translation of Tablet to the Christians, 7
sin, 60, 139
Sinai, Mount, 19, 21, 23, 73–5, 102, 133–5, 137, 154, 162, 184
'slumber', 157
Solomon, 31
Son, the, *see* Christ
Son of Man, 40, 76, 82, 111, 121
soul, 68n
sovereignty, 43, 178
  of Christ, 42
Spirit, the, *see* Christ
Spirit of God, 101
Spirit of Truth, 20, 99–100
  see also Bahá'u'lláh
spirituality, 68, 92, 100, 125, 145–6, 150–3, 158, 187–8, 190
  transcendence of, over worldly pursuits, 108–9
Star of the West, 7
stars, symbolism of, 22, 113–14, 148
steadfastness, 147–8, 190
stones, symbolism of, 105–6, 128
suffering, 188–90
Sunnites, 88
superstition, 139, 140n
Súriy-i-Mulúk, 5
symbolism, 11, 84n, 105–6, 133–4, 159
  of Bible, 30, 106
  of Scriptures, 175–6
  of word 'Tabernacle', 161–2
  of word 'veil', 136–40
Syria, 22, 125–6, 129

Tabernacle, 24, 161–4, 184

Tablet to the Christians (*Lawḥ-i-Aqdas*), 6
  divinely inspired, 30
  English translation of, 7, 13
  published as *Lawh el Akdas: The Holy Tablet*, 7
  published in *Star of the West*, 7
  reason for writing, 34
  recipient of, 6–7
  significance of title of, 8
  style of, 9
  terminology of, 9
  text of, 17–23
  themes of, 8–9
  translations of, 7
  use of biblical Scripture and terminology, 10
Tablets of Bahá'u'lláh, 7
Taherzadeh, Adib, 6–7, 9n, 76, 112
teaching (the Faith), 21, 24, 98, 108, 147–9, 190
teachings of Bahá'u'lláh, 9, 12, 59–60, 63, 76, 78–9, 87, 123, 179, 187
  acceptance of, 131
  a bounty from God, 166
  difficult for Christians to accept, 78
  follower of, a Bahá'í, 188
  listed, 98n
  means for attaining glory, 91–2
  misunderstanding of, 78–9
  obedience to, 184
  practising, 80, 190
  proof of Bahá'u'lláh as a Manifestation, 95
  spiritual transformation through following the, 190
  truth of, 100
  veils to recognition of Bahá'u'lláh, 137
Temple, 161n, 162n, 163
Templers, 58
terminology, explanation of, 9, 11, 30, 86n, 158, 161n

Ṭihrán, 5
transformation, spiritual, 100, 149, 190
truth, 79, 80, 99
  independent investigation of, 20, 63–4, 98, 103–4
  religious, 68n
  spiritual, 100
  triumph over falsehood, 108

understanding, 159, 173
unity, 88
Universal House of Justice, 186n

veils, spiritual, 23, 25, 136–40, 182, 183
Victoria, Queen, 6
violence, 148, 179
virtues, spiritual, *see* spirituality

war, 77
  Second World War, 117, 119
'wealth', 24, 168, 169–70
West, the, 21, 111, 112

Wilhelm I, Kaiser, 6
Will and Testament of 'Abdu'l-Bahá, 185
'Word of God', 25, 38, 59, 77n, 79, 90, 95, 148, 187–9
  'chosen ones' preserve, 166–7
  salvation ensured for those who abide by, 164
  warning against adding to, 99
World Centre, Bahá'í, 37n, 58, 156
world order, 131
writings of Bahá'u'lláh, 37, 178, 181, 186n
  style of, 9
  terminology of, 9–11, 67, 139, 158, 162
  theological content of, 8–11, 79
  understanding of, 190

Zion, 106, 156n
Zoroastrians, 88